A GUIDE FOR FINDING GOD'S HEALING
THROUGH THE COMFORT OF THE PSALMS

RECOVERY
LOSS FROM
AND GRIEF

MICHAEL GIFFORD

GIFFORD PUBLICATIONS

Gifford Publications/
New Heights Marketing, Inc.
Florence, AL
770-606-9195
giffordpublications.com

The
LOSS & GRIEF RECOVERY
Series

Table of Contents

Preface

Loss and grief have many faces

While the loss of a loved one to death is a significant reason for our grief, it's not the only reason. A cherished pet might pass away. We might get laid off or even dismissed from the job that was our primary source of income. Health changes could restrict our ability to move about freely. Divorce could silence the sounds of joy and love that once filled our homes. Any loss has the potential to make us grieve because it separates us from something or someone against our wishes.

It's important for us to acknowledge grief when it enters our lives. In its early stages, it dominates our thoughts, but we don't want it to rule over us for the rest of our days. Acknowledging its existence is the first step on the journey to controlling it.

With that being said, I'd like you to take a few minutes and describe on the lines that follow the loss you have suffered that brought you to this book along with the reasons why you are grieving because of that loss. Certainly, you already know about your loss and your grief over it, but there's a measure of healing that comes with committing your pain to writing. Seeing the description of your sorrow and its cause in your own handwriting makes the situation more real. Of course, you might be saying to yourself, "Aren't these tears that I'm crying and my heart that is breaking enough proof of the reality of what I'm experiencing?" They are indeed sufficient evidence but write down this information anyway and consider it the starting point of your recovery from loss and grief.

You're going to come back to this section of the book from time to time. As the "future you" returns here, read what you wrote on these lines and compare the way you are feeling as the "future you" to how you feel now, as you're completing this section. Hopefully, you will see progress in your recovery.

Here are the lines for you to fill in. Take your time. Keep in mind that this is for your eyes only. You don't need to be an expert writer. Don't hold anything back. Express yourself freely. Use a separate sheet of paper if you run out of room.

Today's Date: _____

Describe your loss on the lines below.

_____

_____

_____

_____

_____

_____

_____

_____

_____

_____

_____

_____

_____

Why are you grieving this loss?

_____

_____

_____

_____

_____

_____

_____

_____

_____

_____

_____

_____

_____

_____

_____

The loss that led to the writing of this book

Now, I'd like to tell you the brief story of my loss that served as the impetus for this book.

It was May 27th. Just one week earlier, my wife, Shannon, had undergone what we had understood was nothing more than routine surgery. I can still see her getting into the van after her follow-up appointment at the doctor's office. She asked me to pull over because we needed to talk. In the next few moments, I would hear the words that everyone dreads as she calmly said, "The doctor told me that I have cancer." At 49 years of age and her at 51, I was not expecting to hear such news. We were "supposed to" enjoy a long life together, walking hand in hand into our winter years, playing with grandchildren, and growing old together. How could it be possible that my wife had developed a disease with the potential to take her away from me far too soon?

As you would expect, tears flowed when we went home and told our children of their mother's diagnosis. We certainly weren't going to give cancer the victory over our spirits or over her life, but we knew that we had a battle ahead of us. Besides that, the mere thought of one whom we loved so much having something wrong with her was unnerving.

Life was relatively calm for about six weeks as we awaited the next surgery. Following it, another month went by without much incident. Then the bottom started to drop out as the cancer spread and began affecting other parts of her body. The next eight months were filled with ambulance rides, hospital stays, emergency room visits, doctor appointments, tests, pills, shots, and a host of procedures and treatments. Finally, just ten months after her diagnosis, Shannon was sent home from the hospital. There was nothing else that could be done other than to make her comfortable in the few weeks the doctors suggested she had left. Less than a year after the day we learned that Shannon had cancer, she went home to be with the Lord. I was with her as she died, holding her hand and gazing intently at the face I would never again see on this side of eternity. Other family members were there as well. Each of us shared our expressions of love with her and she shared hers with us.

Shannon and I exchanged one last loving look into each other's eyes. She then closed her eyes to this world for the final time, only to reopen them in the next world and see the smiling face of the Lord in Paradise. It was a storybook ending to a life well-lived as a wife, a mother, a Bible class teacher, and a faithful Christian who understood what it meant to be a servant to the Lord and to others.

The grief that followed my loss

Like most people, I had suffered multiple losses during the first 50 years of my life. As a pre-teen, I stood with my father at the veterinarian's office as we lovingly stroked the head of our Boston Terrier while she took her last breath. About 18 years later I would get a call telling me that a sudden heart attack had claimed my father's life. Those were extremely difficult, but losing my wife unleashed a more hideous form of grief than I had ever known. This book is available because of that loss. I felt that I had to write it so that others could know about the comfort that God has made available to us all in Psalms. I can't guarantee that this book will help you. However, if you'll take the time to read through the book and meditate on the verses from Psalms, I believe you will benefit because His Word is powerful (Hebrews 4:12).

The layout of this book

This book is designed as a study guide to help you get closer to God as you seek comfort in the midst of loss and grief. It's divided into three parts.

Part One is called "Psalms with Themes of Comfort." It examines twenty-one different Psalms that can bring comfort to the troubled heart. As you can see from the table of contents, I've assigned a theme to each psalm. The purpose of this is to make their contents easier to remember. The themes are only a suggestion. They're not inspired by God.

Each chapter opens with the text of the psalm under consideration, proceeds with a brief examination of that psalm, and closes with thought-provoking questions designed to lead you into further meditation on that psalm and how it applies to your life.

Part Two is entitled "Individual Verses of Comfort." It offers a categorical listing of around 200 verses from the Psalms. I phrased each category in the form of an affirmation and supported each one with a verse or verses from the Psalms. Any of these can be memorized and stored in your heart to ward off grief when it attacks.

Part Three is called "Sitting in the Lap of God." It contains the blog that Shannon and I wrote in the last few months of her life. It includes a great deal of personal material regarding our struggle with cancer. Considering cancer's practically worldwide existence, my hope is that this part will encourage those of you currently fighting a courageous battle against this dreadful disease.

What to expect from this book

You can expect an honest exposition of the Bible verses cited. Since the book spotlights the Bible as the ultimate source of comfort, to misrepresent or misapply the passages under consideration would be misleading. In addition, as a teacher of God's Word, I have a responsibility to speak the truth (James 3:1) and to do it in love (Ephesians 4:15).

You can expect to find numerous Bible references. The focus is the book of Psalms, but there are many other passages from God's Word that support the statements made in the Psalms. Whenever I could, I used Bible verses to help illustrate and explain other Bible verses.

You can expect some moments of sadness along with the moments of comfort. The times of sadness are not necessarily setbacks in the recovery process. A loss can strike deeply into our hearts. The grief that follows the loss can rear its head at some of the most unusual times. A sound, a smell, or even some words you read on a page of this book can ignite your grief as these things remind you of your loss. Don't be discouraged. Recovery from loss and grief can't be measured with a stopwatch. We all grieve differently and in our own time.

With the Psalms as our guide, I invite you to join me now on the road to recovery from loss and grief. Each of the psalms we'll be considering helped me immensely as I grieved my loss. My prayer is that you will also find the comfort that you are craving.

Michael Gifford

Part One
Psalms with Themes of Comfort

Introduction to Part One

When faced with life's challenges, the afflicted individual often measures the words of comfort from friends and family by this one primary thought: "Have you felt what I'm feeling now?" While another's warm touch, sympathizing tear, and gentle word can indeed help the troubled soul, there is nothing like talking to someone who has "been there." God demonstrated His understanding of this principle by sending Jesus to take on a fleshly body. "For since He Himself was tempted in that which He has suffered, He is able to come to the aid of those who are tempted." (Hebrews 2:18). In the Psalms, God inspired His writers to occasionally tell us something of the depths of their sorrows and struggles. These were not men spouting empty platitudes from ivory towers. Each one of them had waged a personal war against despair, poured forth the tears of anguish, and begged from shattered hearts for comfort from the Father.

How many of us have ever cried like this:

> I am weary with my sighing; Every night I make my bed swim,
> I dissolve my couch with my tears. My eye has wasted away
> with grief; It has become old because of all my adversaries.
> (Psalm 6:6-7).

This was not the intermittent shedding of tears brought about by moments of sadness. This was, as we might say today, "bawling your eyes out." David's crying was so intense that it had literally drained him of physical strength. His vision was diminished by the cloudiness of the tears. The severity of his heartache was so great that crying alone could not express it. Groans flowed from his lips in unison with the tears. If you have hurt like David, then you know how he felt. Perhaps your tears have been so strong that your stomach ached or your head hurt. Perhaps your crying had so weakened you that you could not eat. Perhaps you even cried yourself to sleep. You have a friend in the inspired Psalmist, for even if the cause of his suffering might not have been the same as yours, he was well acquainted with sorrow's tears.

Closely connected to the Psalmists' tears were their feelings of being overwhelmed by their circumstances. Psalm 69 begins:

> Save me, O God, For the waters have threatened my life. I have sunk in deep mire, and there is no foothold; I have come into deep waters, and a flood overflows me. (verses 1-2).

This is a poignant verbal picture of someone who feels like he has lost control. Not only is he being pulled down by the undertow of the rivers of sorrow, but the dike of protection has burst and the flood waters of despair have come crashing down on top of him. He has no footing but is sinking deeper and deeper into the mire.

When you first learned of your loss, did it feel that everything started coming at you at once? When earlier in life, perhaps just a few days or hours earlier, everything was running smoothly and pleasantly, suddenly you found yourself being bombarded on every side with emotions, thoughts, and new directions in life that heretofore would have never even crossed your mind. Maybe your mind became so overloaded that you could barely think straight. Perhaps conversations with others were like dreams filled with empty words that passed over your head and never touched your ears. So much began happening all at once that you might have felt those overwhelming waters of Psalm 69 rushing over your head.

In many of the Psalms we find the writers turning immediately to God, praising and honoring Him. In some of them, however, while they eventually turned to God, initially they expressed concerns about God's care for them. The inspired writer of Psalm 13 opened this particular poem with the questions:

> How long, O Lord? Will You forget me forever? How long will You hide Your face from me?

Had God deserted this writer? He certainly had not, but in the Psalmist's anguish, he felt that the One on whom he had learned to depend had in fact turned His back on the trouble and forgotten His servant. Why doesn't God answer? Why did He let this happen to me? What possible good can come from all of this? Such expressions are as evident in the hearts of sufferers today as they were when this Psalmist penned his questions.

Is there anyone who, in their grief, has not at least once asked, "Why?" This simple, one-word question is not necessarily a challenge to God, nor is it necessarily an indication of a lack of faith. It could instead be a reflection of our imperfection and our inability to see and fully know the mind of God. It's possible that on earth we may never fully know why. That's where faith comes in. We don't know why, but we have faith that God does, and we trust Him to lead us through the darkness of our grief.

Much more could be said about the depths of despair from which the Psalmists often wrote, but in these few short paragraphs, we can see in these men's lives an affirmative answer to the question with which this chapter opened: "Have you felt what I'm feeling now?" Indeed, they did experience these feelings, and in writing by perfect inspiration of the Holy Spirit, they have shown their words to be worthy of our consideration as we seek the comfort from the Lord that lifted them from their sorrows.

The circumstances behind each Psalm may be different from ours, but the pain is just as real. It may not be death or illness that triggers our sorrow. There are countless difficulties in life that could prompt tears and heartache. The fact is, however, that every sorrow bears the same characteristic; it hurts. No matter what has caused our hearts to become heavy, even if it's something that might seem trivial to others, it still hurts and we still want relief. In reading these Psalms, we can see others who themselves felt this pain. In studying their inspired words, it's as though we were walking hand in hand with them, facing life's troubles with them, and looking up with them for the comfort that they found and that we ourselves can find in the Lord.

Key Takeaways from the Introduction to Part One
• The Psalms were written by the inspiration of God by men who had themselves experienced loss and grief. • Like us, the writers of the Psalms sometimes felt overwhelmed by their troubles. • We may never know why things happen in our lives, but God does.

Moments of Meditation

1. What is hurting you most about your loss?

_____

_____

_____

_____

_____

2. How might talking to someone who has been through what you're going through help you handle your loss?

_____

_____

_____

_____

3. List the names of three people you know who have suffered a loss similar to yours and then contact them to ask if they would be willing to talk to you about it.

_____

_____

_____

4. What, if anything, is making you feel overwhelmed by your loss?

_____

_____

_____

_____

5. Are you feeling abandoned by God or loved by Him at this time? Why do you feel that way?

_____

_____

_____

_____

If you're feeling overwhelmed, try making a check list. Write down on separate lines everything that needs to be done. Then go back and label every task as either "Needs to be done today," "Needs to be done within the next 7 days," or "Needs to be done within the next month." Get three different colors of highlighters and give each of the three options a different color. Check off the tasks as they are completed. Actually seeing what you need to get done helps you be organized which, in turn, reduces stress. Checking them off is encouraging because it helps you see your progress.

Chapter One
Psalm 1
The Comfort of Stability

[1] How blessed is the man who does not walk in the counsel of the wicked, nor stand in the path of sinners, nor sit in the seat of scoffers!

[2] But his delight is in the law of the LORD, and in His law he meditates day and night.

[3] He will be like a tree *firmly* planted by streams of water, which yields its fruit in its season and its leaf does not wither; and in whatever he does, he prospers.

[4] The wicked are not so, but they are like chaff which the wind drives away.

[5] Therefore the wicked will not stand in the judgment, nor sinners in the assembly of the righteous.

[6] For the LORD knows the way of the righteous, but the way of the wicked will perish.

Examination of the Psalm

How appropriate that this first Psalm opens with the word, "blessed" or "happy." Through powerful illustrations and statements, it declares that this happiness is found in stability.

The third verse paints a picture of stability for us as it describes a healthy and prosperous tree. Notice that this is not a tree that has grown wild, nor is it one that has sprung from a mere scattering of seed from a farmer's hand. This tree has been carefully planted. Furthermore, it has been planted thoughtfully and purposefully in a location that is well-watered, thus giving it the best opportunity to be productive. Its roots push deeply into the rich soil and ground it firmly. As it gains strength in its foundation, it bears fruit in abundance and does not wither or fade, even during the stress of the hottest of days, the bitterest of wintry temperatures, or the harshest of winds. It is steadfast and unshakeable.

The fourth verse again demonstrates stability, but from a negative perspective. Here, the picture is of a farmer winnowing his grain. He tosses the grain into the air and while the heavier kernels fall to the ground, the lighter husks or chaff are carried away by the wind. While the emphasis in the verse is on the chaff that is blown away, the analogy bears the implication that there were also desirable grains that were landing where they were supposed to. Instability is pictured in the chaff and soundness and positive expectations are pictured in the kernels of the grain.

Yet another reference to stability is found in the sixth verse in which the Psalmist speaks of the Lord knowing the way of the righteous. One fact is certain when loss and grief come into our lives: We are traveling a new and unknown path. To be sure, we might have faced similar situations in the past, but no two challenges are exactly alike. For example, while the loss of a parent to death is bitterly painful, no one can begin to compare it to the loss of a spouse. While the death of a spouse brings unspeakable sorrow, no one can compare it to the loss of a child. It's not possible for anyone to rank one form of sorrow as being worse than another. The point is that each difficulty carries its own weight of heartache and grief. Each is a new experience. Each is an unknown way for us as humans, but "the Lord knows the way of the righteous." God knows the way. He is the constant in the uncertainty that loss brings with it.

The aforementioned verses show that stability truly exists. Further, we can enjoy this stability, even while wrestling with life's most formidable challenges. But does stability show itself voluntarily without any effort on our part? Can we expect to be standing in the darkest of despair's shadows one day and automatically be catapulted by some unknown force into the brightest of life's joys the next?

Look again at verse three and notice that this entire verse shows a result. It depicts the end of a means. The means is found in verses one and two. The person described in those two verses is one who does not walk in the counsel of the wicked, does not stand in the path of sinners, and does not sit in the seat of scoffers. This individual does, however, take delight in meditating on the law of the Lord day and night. This is why he is like a tree planted by the rivers of water. He seeks God and loves His Word. Although there are things in life that threaten his fruitfulness and spiritual prosperity, he enjoys stability because he is firmly grounded in the one true God, who Himself is the essence of stability. Just as the farmer purposefully planted the tree in a rich and beneficial location, the individual who enjoys God's stability has purposefully planted himself or herself in the rich and spiritually beneficial firm foundation of God's inspired Word.

Now look again at verse four. Who is blown away like the chaff? Who will never know the stability that God offers through His Word? It is the ungodly man or woman. They cannot stand, and will not stand, because they are unstable. In fact, verse five clearly shows that those who turn away from God have no foundation at all. When their world quakes uncontrollably, they have nothing solid to grasp because their ungodly foundation is the cause of their instability.

Application

In the summer of 1988, I was participating in a Bible lectureship in the Pacific Islands. During one of the lectures the ground began to rumble and the structures started to shake. For the first time in my life, I was experiencing an earthquake. The locals, having endured these disturbances countless times, probably enjoyed the entertainment of watching at least this one American frantically scanning the area for something to grab for support. They knew full well, as I myself soon realized, that nothing above the ground could provide stability as long as the ground itself was quaking uncontrollably. The very foundation upon which we stood having become unstable, we could not expect anything that rested upon this faulty foundation to be trustworthy.

When loss and grief invade our lives, we can easily identify with the feeling of helplessness that comes with being in an earthquake. Things are no longer as they once were. The shaky, temporal nature of this earthly life is never more evident than when trials beset us. We can stretch with all of our might in an effort to grab hold of something here on earth that is rock solid and immovable, but we will only grasp air. Where is the stability that we so desperately crave when our world is crumbling? Where is that constant to which we can cling when the tides of sorrow are threatening to sweep us away? Is it even possible for us to regain our balance or are we doomed to live a life of continual sadness and despair?

Our stability depends upon us turning to God because He is stability defined. Consider these characteristics of His stability:

- He is eternal (Psalm 90:2), which means He was in existence before the world began.

- He was there in the beginning of the world, He Himself being the Creator (Genesis 1).

- He is ever present each second, He Himself being the sustainer of His creation (Jeremiah 23:23-24).

- He will be there at the end of the world, He Himself being the One who will destroy the elements (2 Peter 3:10-12) and judge mankind (Matthew 25:31-46).

- He was there when the Bible began to be written (2 Timothy 3:16-17).

- He gave each word of the Bible to His inspired writers (1 Corinthians 2:7-15).

- He will be there in the end to employ His Word in judgment (Revelation 20:12).

- He was there at the beginning of each of our lives (Psalm 139:13).

- He is with us on a moment-by-moment basis (Hebrews 13:5).

- He will be with us at the end of our days (Psalm 23).

- Daily, He is there when we rise in the morning (Psalm 5:3), He is there with us throughout the day (Matthew 6:25-34), He is there with us when the day is done (Psalm 4:8), and then He is there with us all through the night (Psalm 121:4).

God's stability is demonstrated in His faithfulness to mankind and is seen throughout the Bible.

- His faithfulness to us is found in Genesis where we learn of mankind's fall into sin followed immediately by the introduction of God's plan for redeeming man (Genesis 3:15).

- It's found throughout the rest of the books of the Law, from Exodus to Deuteronomy, where we read of God delivering Israel from Egyptian bondage and leading that nation to the earthly promised land of Canaan. The record of this journey is a beautiful foreshadowing of the Christian's walk through the wilderness of this world to the eternal promised land of heaven.

- It's in the Old Testament books of history, from Joshua through Esther, where God is constantly involved in the affairs of Israel and Judah.

- It's in the books of poetry from Job to Song of Solomon in which inspired writers tell us of God's deliverance and dependability.

- It's in the words of the Old Testament prophets, from Isaiah through Malachi, where one inspired man after another continues the theme of eternal redemption begun in Genesis by foretelling the coming of the Messiah to pay the price for the sins of mankind.

- It's in the Gospel accounts of the New Testament where we read of the actual physical arrival of Jesus, God in the flesh (John 1:14), His perfect life, and His death, burial, and resurrection.

- It's in the book of Acts where we find men like Stephen finding the Lord faithful to him even in death (Acts 7).

- It's in the New Testament epistles, from Romans through Jude, in which we find an abundance of precious promises all given by our God who cannot lie (Titus 1:2).

- It's in the book of Revelation and its powerful portrait of victory in heaven for the faithful, provided by the One whose "words are faithful and true" (Revelation 22:6).

We can have the stability that brings comfort when it seems our world is falling to pieces. We can be the firmly planted tree and the weighted grain. We can walk confidently upon the shifting sands of life if we are walking with the One who knows the way.

Key Takeaways from Chapter 1

- God is the source of true stability in our lives.
- No matter how unfamiliar we are with loss and grief, we can take comfort in the fact that God knows the way.
- We must walk faithfully with God in order to enjoy His stability.

Moments of Meditation

1. Why do you want stability in your life?

   _____

   _____

   _____

2. On a scale of 1 to 5, with 1 being "not at all" and 5 being "very," how stable is your life at this time?

   _____

3. What is the reason for your answer in #2?

   _____

   _____

_____

_____

4. What did the Psalmist mean when he wrote, "But his delight is in the law of the LORD, and in His law he meditates day and night"?

_____

_____

_____

_____

5. How does the truth that "the Lord knows the way of the righteous" bring you comfort and peace, especially during times of uncertainty?

_____

_____

_____

_____

Be sure to take care of yourself physically. Loss and grief can seriously disrupt your routine. At times, you might find yourself not eating or sleeping like you should. At other times, you might sleep more than usual or eat practically everything in sight.

If you notice, or a friend notices, a change in your eating and sleeping habits, try creating a daily health journal to help you track these two activities.

- Start by taking note of what your typical eating and sleeping patterns were prior to your loss and grief.

- Next, close each day by writing down what you've eaten and how much you've slept that day.

- After a week of keeping these records, review your journal. You should be able to detect patterns. Make note of unusual trends.

- Finish the day by writing down your goals for sleeping that night (for example, "My goal is to sleep for eight hours tonight.") and creating a healthy meal plan for the next day.

- Continue to write in your daily health journal as long as is needed.

Chapter Two
Psalm 3
Comfort in the Strength
and Protection of God

[1] O LORD, how my adversaries have increased! Many are rising up against me.

[2] Many are saying of my soul, "There is no deliverance for him in God." *Selah.*

[3] But You, O LORD, are a shield about me, my glory, and the One who lifts my head.

[4] I was crying to the LORD with my voice, and He answered me from His holy mountain. *Selah.*

[5] I lay down and slept; I awoke, for the LORD sustains me.

[6] I will not be afraid of ten thousands of people who have set themselves against me round about.

[7] Arise, O LORD; save me, O my God! For You have smitten all my enemies on the cheek; You have shattered the teeth of the wicked.

[8] Salvation belongs to the LORD; Your blessing *be* upon Your people! *Selah.*

Examination of the Psalm

The caption of this Psalm, though not Divinely inspired, suggests that it was written by King David when he fled from his son, Absalom. A full account of this can be found in 2 Samuel, chapters 15 through 18. In essence, Absalom deceived the Israelites and caused David to be run out of the land (2 Samuel 15:13-14). David's own son turned the people against the mighty king. The sixth verse of this Psalm might be hyperbole, but then again perhaps it's not such a stretch to imagine Absalom having poisoned tens of thousands of hearts against David.

Verses six and seven form the basis for the claim that this is a psalm of comfort. Considering his circumstances, how could David possibly sleep well at night and walk without fear during the day? Aren't panic and desperation often associated with the onslaught of troubles? Aren't worry and doubt those insidious thieves that typically rob us of sleep and inner peace when we're faced with difficulties? These were not a part of David's mindset, however, for he knew that the God of all creation was taking care of him. Even though his enemies had "increased," were "many" in number, and were even mocking him, saying, "There is no deliverance for him in God," this sweet psalmist of Israel (2 Samuel 23:1) enjoyed peace of mind. Though his detractors should gang up in the tens of thousands against him, David would not fear because his trust was in the all-powerful God. No matter how many rose up against him, he knew he would be the victor with his hand in the hand of the Lord.

In verse three, David portrays God as a shield. The words, "But You, O Lord, are a shield about me," indicate that God had covered him with protection. In the same verse, the writer refers to God as "my glory." Even though this phrase is explained in various ways, it seems that since David was honoring God in the context, he was indicating that God was the source of his glory or honor. Being that source, He could be counted on to care for David regardless of the severity of the attacks that might be aimed at him.

Again, in verse three, David identifies God as "the One who lifts my head." This could have referred to God keeping David's head up in hope rather than down in despair or it could have been a prophecy of David's return to power in Israel. In either case, the Lord was the One who had the strength to accomplish these tasks. It was his confidence in this Divine strength that prompted David to cry out to the Lord and it was his knowledge of God having heard his cry that led to his restful nights and fear-free days.

Application

Have you ever had tens of thousands of people chasing after you? Have you ever been so beset by enemies that you had to run for your life? Perhaps not, but if you have experienced difficulties in your life, you are familiar with the feeling that practically everything and everyone is against you.

Have you ever made these comments to yourself? "Nothing ever goes my way." "Nothing ever works out for me." "It's not fair." "This isn't supposed to be happening to me." Real or imagined, these feelings hurt and can lead to the worry and doubt mentioned earlier. Is there anything we can do about our situation? Is there anyone who can help us? Yes, there is a shield and "lifter up of the head" who demonstrates His strength to protect just as powerfully as he did in the days of king David.

The last nine verses of the eighth chapter of Romans go hand in hand with the message of God's protection in the third Psalm. Together these verses form a beautiful segment of inspired Scripture that remind us of the amazing ability of our God to provide the strength we need in times of trouble.

In the context, Paul is writing in regard to suffering being experienced by Christians in Rome. Romans 8:31 asks, "What then shall we say to these things? If God is for us, who is against us?" Immediately we see the power of God in these two simple questions. No matter how great the challenges of life may become, nothing can capture and enslave us if we are walking with God. None of life's tribulations can rule our hearts when our hearts are shielded by the Lord.

Reading on, we find Paul reminding Christians of the extent to which God had gone to show His loving care. He had given His only begotten Son. This is called an argument from the greater to the lesser. Since God was willing to send Jesus to die for the sins of mankind, why should we think that He would not take care of and protect us on a daily basis?

Then Paul comes to his magnificent conclusion. Read it, memorize it, internalize it, and let these Divinely inspired words lead you through the dark valley of life's challenges.

Who will separate us from the love of Christ? Will tribulation, or distress, or persecution, or famine, or nakedness, or peril, or sword? Just as it is written, "For Your sake we are being put to death all day long; we were considered as sheep to be

17

slaughtered." But in all these things we overwhelmingly conquer through Him who loved us. For I am convinced that neither death, nor life, nor angels, nor principalities, nor things present, nor things to come, nor powers, nor height, nor depth, nor any other created thing, will be able to separate us from the love of God, which is in Christ Jesus our Lord. (Romans 8:35-39).

Satan would have us believe that there is no help in God. He would raise tens of thousands of doubts and distresses in our minds. God is our strength and protection against the fiery darts of the devil (Ephesians 6:16). Like David, we too can say in our trials, "The Lord sustains (supports, M.G.) me."

Key Takeaways from Chapter 2

- God is stronger than our troubles.
- We can sleep peacefully knowing that God is a shield for the faithful.
- If God is for us, who is against us?

Moments of Meditation

1. How does God put a shield around us?

_____

_____

_____

_____

_____

_____

2. What, if anything, is discouraging you the most at this time?

_____

_____

_____

_____

_____

3. In what ways is this source of discouragement hurting you?

_____

_____

_____

_____

_____

4. List three action steps that you can take to make the discouragement go away.

_____

_____

_____

_____

_____

_____

5. What did Paul mean when he wrote, "If God is for us, who is against us?"

_____

_____

_____

_____

If your grief is due to the death of a loved one, it's possible that you feel that you left some things unsaid. Try writing a letter to your loved one. It's an excellent way to relieve pent-up emotions.

Chapter Three
Psalm 22
Comfort in the Messianic Promise

[1] My God, my God, why have You forsaken me? Far from my deliverance are the words of my groaning.

[2] O my God, I cry by day, but You do not answer; and by night, but I have no rest.

[3] Yet You are holy, O You who are enthroned upon the praises of Israel.

[4] In You our fathers trusted; they trusted and You delivered them.

[5] To You they cried out and were delivered; in You they trusted and were not disappointed.

[6] But I am a worm and not a man, a reproach of men and despised by the people.

[7] All who see me sneer at me; they separate with the lip, they wag the head, *saying*,

[8] "Commit *yourself* to the LORD; let Him deliver him; Let Him rescue him, because He delights in him."

[9] Yet You are He who brought me forth from the womb; You made me trust *when* upon my mother's breasts.

[10] Upon You I was cast from birth; You have been my God from my mother's womb.

[11] Be not far from me, for trouble is near; for there is none to help.

[12] Many bulls have surrounded me; strong *bulls* of Bashan have encircled me.

[13] They open wide their mouth at me, as a ravening and a roaring lion.

14 I am poured out like water, and all my bones are out of joint; my heart is like wax; it is melted within me.

[15] My strength is dried up like a potsherd, and my tongue cleaves to my jaws; and You lay me in the dust of death.

[16] For dogs have surrounded me; a band of evildoers has encompassed me; they pierced my hands and my feet.

¹⁷ I can count all my bones. They look, they stare at me;

¹⁸ They divide my garments among them, and for my clothing they cast lots.

¹⁹ But You, O LORD, be not far off; O You my help, hasten to my assistance.

²⁰ Deliver my soul from the sword, my only *life* from the power of the dog.

²¹ Save me from the lion's mouth; from the horns of the wild oxen You answer me.

²² I will tell of Your name to my brethren; in the midst of the assembly I will praise You.

²³ You who fear the LORD, praise Him; all you descendants of Jacob, glorify Him, and stand in awe of Him, all you descendants of Israel.

²⁴ For He has not despised nor abhorred the affliction of the afflicted; nor has He hidden His face from him; but when he cried to Him for help, He heard.

²⁵ From You *comes* my praise in the great assembly; I shall pay my vows before those who fear Him.

²⁶ The afflicted will eat and be satisfied; those who seek Him will praise the LORD. Let your heart live forever!

²⁷ All the ends of the earth will remember and turn to the LORD, and all the families of the nations will worship before You.

²⁸ For the kingdom is the LORD's and He rules over the nations.

²⁹ All the prosperous of the earth will eat and worship, all those who go down to the dust will bow before Him, even he who cannot keep his soul alive.

³⁰ Posterity will serve Him; it will be told of the LORD to the *coming* generation.

³¹ They will come and will declare His righteousness to a people who will be born, that He has performed it.

Examination of the Psalm

The comfort we receive from the Lord while here on earth is tremendous. Psalm 94:19 says, "When my anxious thoughts multiply within me, Your consolations delight my soul." The hearts and minds of faithful Christians are sustained daily by God's great mercy and care. Beyond this earthly realm, however, is eternal comfort. Thoughts of eternity with God elicit moments of peace as we contemplate the land beyond where "there will no longer be any death; there will no longer be any mourning, or crying, or pain; the first things have passed away" (Revelation 21:4). The ultimate comfort is heaven. This Psalm prophesies of the One whose suffering and death opened the way to heaven so that we can enjoy this hope here on earth and peace and comfort in eternity.

The Psalm opens with a plaintive cry from one whose anguish is so deep that he considers that God has turned a blind eye to his pain and a deaf ear to his pleas for help. His calamitous state is further seen in verses 6-8 and 16-18. Were this just the writer himself bemoaning his sorrowful situation, we would be sufficiently touched to feel for him and pity his poor condition. However, when we come to the New Testament and find that these verses are prophecies of none other than Jesus Christ Himself during His suffering up to and while on the cross, we realize the depth of the heartache felt by our Lord while He walked the earth in human flesh. That He Himself suffered is enough to make us weep, but that He suffered due to no sin of His own is not only enough to make us weep, but also to thank God for the temporal suffering Jesus endured so that we might avoid eternal suffering in hell.

The Messianic prophecies of Psalm 22 find their fulfillment in the events recorded in the books of Matthew, Mark, Luke, and John.

- Psalm 22:1 is uttered by Jesus while He hung on the cross (Matthew 27:46; Mark 15:34).

- Psalm 22:6-8 describes in perfect prophetic fashion the surrounding scene of human indecency as Jesus was giving His life's blood for our sins (Matthew 27:39-44; Mark 15:29-32; Luke 23:35-37).

- Psalm 22:16 foretells the piercing of the Christ (Matthew 27:35; Mark 15:25; Luke 23:33; John 19:18; 20:24-27).

- Psalm 22:17-18 gives more details regarding the actions of the onlookers at the cross (Matthew 27:35; Mark 15:24; Luke 23:34).

These verses are just a few of many Old Testament prophecies regarding the sacrificial death of the Messiah. Just as some reject Him today, some in the days of the apostle Paul rejected the idea of a suffering Messiah. "But we preach Christ crucified, to Jews a stumbling block and to Gentiles foolishness, but to those who are the called, both Jews and Greeks, Christ the power of God and the wisdom of God." (1 Corinthians 1:23-24). Their unbelief notwithstanding, the necessity of the sacrifice of Christ is clearly seen.

> But we do see Him who was made for a little while lower than the angels, namely, Jesus, because of the suffering of death crowned with glory and honor, so that by the grace of God He might taste death for everyone. (Hebrews 2:9).

Sinful man cannot atone for his own sins. God's perfect justice (Deuteronomy 32:4) could only be satisfied by the sacrifice of the sinless Messiah (1 Peter 2:21-24).

> Knowing that you were not redeemed with perishable things like silver or gold from your futile way of life inherited from your forefathers, but with precious blood, as of a lamb unblemished and spotless, the blood of Christ. (1 Peter 1:18-19).

That sinless Messiah was God in the flesh (John 1:1,14), Jesus Christ.

Application

Having devoted space to a discussion of the Messianic prophecies of Psalm 22 and their fulfillment in Jesus, we now take time to explain how all of this serves as a source of comfort. There are two important points.

First, the agony experienced by the Messiah reminds us that our Lord is deeply familiar with human suffering. He wept with the family of deceased Lazarus who mourned the loss of their loved one (John 11:35). He was saddened by the unfaithfulness of those whom He came to seek and to save (Luke 19:10,41). He was betrayed by a friend (Matthew

24

26:14-16). His closest confidants forsook Him in His hour of trial (Mark 14:50). As Isaiah prophesied of Him, Jesus was "despised and forsaken of men, a man of sorrows and acquainted with grief…" (Isaiah 53:3). When we say that the Lord understands our troubles, we genuinely and literally mean that He understands our troubles for He Himself met life's difficulties face to face as a man. As is written in Hebrews 4:14-16,

> Therefore, since we have a great high priest who has passed through the heavens, Jesus the Son of God, let us hold fast our confession. For we do not have a high priest who cannot sympathize with our weaknesses, but One who has been tempted in all things as we are, yet without sin. Therefore let us draw near with confidence to the throne of grace, so that we may receive mercy and find grace to help in time of need.

No matter how deeply our hearts may hurt, in the Bible we have the words of the One who walked life's perilous path and in prayer we can go to the Father through Him (1 Timothy 2:5).

Secondly, the suffering of the Savior reminds us to keep our earthly troubles in perspective. This life is not all there is. King Solomon wrote of man going "to his eternal home" (Ecclesiastes 12:5). Two verses later he said, "Then the dust will return to the earth as it was: and the spirit will return to God who gave it" (Ecclesiastes 12:7). Regardless of the duration of any suffering we might experience, its length pales in comparison to eternity. We are all steadily marching toward the end of this life and the beginning of the next. Peter wrote, "All flesh is like grass, and all its glory like the flower of grass. The grass withers, and the flower falls off, but the word of the Lord endures forever" (1 Peter 1:24). Hebrews 9:27 reads, "…it is appointed for men to die once and after this comes judgment." This is a sobering thought and would indeed be most disturbing and depressing had it not been for that suffering Savior who paid the price for sin so that those who obey Him could face life's difficulties with the hope of heaven in their hearts. Because of the blood of Christ, a faithful Christian can view life's challenges from the perspective of one who knows that these troubles are temporary rather than eternal. He or she can face troubles with assurance of eternal relief because Christ entered "into heaven itself, now to appear in the presence of God for us" (Hebrews 9:24).

Psalm 22 is indeed a remarkable reminder of the eternal comfort awaiting the faithful as a result of the suffering and ultimately victorious Messiah, Jesus Christ.

> And I heard a voice from heaven, saying, Write, Blessed are the dead who die in the Lord from now on! Yes, says the Spirit, so that they may rest from their labors, for their deeds follow with them. (Revelation 14:13).

Key Takeaways from Chapter 3

- Jesus knows what it's like to suffer as a human.
- Our earthly troubles are only temporary.
- Jesus made it possible for us to have eternal comfort in heaven through His death on the cross.

Moments of Meditation

1. Why did God send Jesus to die for us?

_____

_____

_____

_____

_____

2. Why did Jesus come to earth in the flesh?

_____

_____

_____

_____

_____

3. Hebrews 4:15 says that Jesus was "tempted in all things as we are, yet without sin." Do you find that to be comforting? If so, why?

_____

_____

_____

_____

_____

4. Jesus' friends abandoned Him when He needed them most. Do you feel that your friends have abandoned you or do you feel that they are trying to help you?

_____

_____

_____

_____

_____

5. How do thoughts of heaven comfort you in your loss and grief?

_____

_____

_____

_____

_____

Loss and grief are real. Furthermore, they are not limited to the death of a loved one. It's not unusual to feel grief over the loss of a job, the loss of health, the loss of a pet, or the loss of a relationship. Don't be afraid or ashamed to acknowledge that you have suffered a loss. Likewise, don't be afraid or ashamed to ask for help in dealing with your loss and grief.

Chapter Four
Psalm 23
The Comfort of Realizing that the Shepherd Knows Me and I Know the Shepherd

[1] The LORD is my shepherd, I shall not want.
[2] He makes me lie down in green pastures; He leads me beside quiet waters.
[3] He restores my soul; He guides me in the paths of righteousness for His name's sake.
[4] Even though I walk through the valley of the shadow of death, I fear no evil, for You are with me; Your rod and Your staff, they comfort me.
[5] You prepare a table before me in the presence of my enemies; You have anointed my head with oil; My cup overflows.
[6] Surely goodness and lovingkindness will follow me all the days of my life, and I will dwell in the house of the LORD forever.

Examination of the Psalm

When it comes to providing comfort for the troubled soul, certainly no section of Sacred Scripture has been read more often than the twenty-third Psalm. The single sentence in verse four has no doubt consoled untold millions of breaking hearts as they watched the remains of their deceased loved ones being lowered into the earth or as they themselves confronted their own mortality. The very thought of having the Divine Shepherd lead His sheep into the unknown realms of eternity is enough to soothe the most troubled mind if we are following Him as our guide. Still, for all that this Psalm means to us as we contemplate death, its value as a source of comfort is much broader.

This psalm is so rich and deep that entire books have been devoted to comments on it. There is no way that I can treat every precious facet of its meaning in just one chapter. That being the case, I want to focus on just one aspect of the Psalm, namely, the emphasis in the Psalm on the personal relationship between the Shepherd and the sheep.

Even a brief reading of the Psalm clearly shows that David, the inspired penman, is writing from the perspective of the sheep. Having once been a shepherd himself (1 Samuel 16:11), he no doubt would have well understood the role of the shepherd and the needs of the sheep. Throughout the Psalm he uses the physical shepherd/sheep relationship to illustrate that which exists between God, the Divine Shepherd and those who faithfully follow Him through His Word.

The Psalmist inserts a personal pronoun into every verse. "I shall not want…" "He makes me lie down…" "He restores my soul…" In the New American Standard Bible of 1995 there are 114 words in the Psalm. Of those, 17 are pronouns referring to the Psalmist himself. The Psalm opens and closes by identifying "the Lord" as the object of the inspired writer's affection. In between those verses, he repeatedly demonstrates that it is this Lord who is taking care of him, as 10 times he uses the pronouns "he," "his," "your" and "you." In essence, even though the great and mighty God is the master of all creation (Genesis 1), He still cares for His people individually and allows us to know Him on an intimate basis (1 John 2:1-5). Any and every faithful child of God can say, "The Shepherd knows me and I know the Shepherd."

Suppose your favorite musician was performing in a huge outdoor stadium. Being such a loyal fan, you would be there with ticket in hand to join the tens of thousands of others who admire this talented individual. Now suppose that you've taken your seat among the screaming masses. The musician steps onto the stage and as he looks out over the packed stadium he spots you. He then promptly proceeds to the microphone and calls you by name to come down and see him. Can you begin to imagine how thrilled you would be? Here is this world-renowned musician singling you out by name in a crowd of upwards to a hundred thousand fans. It wouldn't even matter to you how he knew your name. Just knowing that he knew you and knowing that everyone in that stadium knew that he knew you would be incredible.

It's sad but true that what often excites us in the physical realm does nothing for us in the spiritual realm; yet to have the assurance that God as my Shepherd knows me personally is comfort beyond compare. As David brings out so beautifully in this Psalm, the Shepherd Divine doesn't just know about me. He knows ME and He knows my every need. It's because of this that "I shall not want." I will never be in need of anything. My Shepherd knows what is best for me and He will readily provide all that I require. By giving concrete examples of the Shepherd's knowledge of and provision for the needs of His sheep, the next two verses expound on the fact that because "the Lord is my Shepherd, I shall not want."

"He makes me lie down in green pastures." God knows that we need emotional rest. He knows we need and want to be at peace. He also knows that the uncertainties of life can bring about worry and distress that can destroy inner peace. A sheep that is agitated by danger, disease, hunger or thirst will not lie down. Only in the abundance of pastures of tender grass will it feel content enough to not only lie down, but to rest comfortably. Through prayer, in which He allows us to cast our cares upon Him (1 Peter 5:7) and through His written Word, by which our faith is established and strengthened (Romans 10:17), God has given us the green pastures in which we can relax and repose.

Notice just the words, "green pastures" in verse two. The shepherd will give his sheep a place to lie down. But where will it be? Will he lead them to dry, cracked, rock-covered clay much like what we see in the southern United States in the summer? No, he will lead them to the green pastures where his sheep can eat their fill and then lie down in the cool, soothing grass. He will give them his best. So it is with God the Shepherd. He offers us the best; the greenest of pastures, the highest of hopes, the pinnacle of peace, the zenith of comfort. No matter the level of our stresses, our hearts can be calm because our God knows our need for rest and peace and, what's more, He provides these blessings in abundance. Being plural, the word "pastures" suggests ongoing provision. Wherever there is a green pasture, the shepherd will take his sheep there. God doesn't offer us a crumb here and a morsel there. In Psalm 81:10, the Lord said, "open your mouth wide and I will fill it."

Psalm 23:5 speaks of the overflowing nature of God's blessings. Ephesians 3:20-21 reads, "Now to Him who is able to do far more abundantly beyond all that we ask or think, according to the power that works within us, to Him be the glory in the church and in Christ Jesus to all generations forever and ever. Amen." We will never exhaust the blessings of God.

"He leads me beside quiet waters." Now the sheep is thirsty. Does the shepherd lead it to the raging rapids and force it in? Of course not. He leads his sheep to "waters of quietness" as the alternate rendering of this phrase in the King James Version reads. If the maxim, "still waters run deep" holds true, then we can see that this watering hole is not only a place of peacefulness, but it is also a place of plenty as the water source is deep enough for the sheep to be able to drink its fill. As he has done in the first half of the verse, David is illustrating God's knowledge of the needs of His sheep and His abundant provision for them.

"He restores my soul" is a continuation of the thought presented in verse two. This is a beautiful statement that lends itself to the idea that he (the shepherd) brings the sheep back to life. The sheep is weary and thirsty due to its wandering. In providing for the needs of the sheep, the shepherd not only refreshes it, but also restores it. The word "restores" indicates continuous action. "He continually restores my soul." This is the case whenever we are distressed and seek God as the singular solution for our sadness. The world and its circumstances wear us down. We seek God through prayer and His written Word and every time we do, He continually restores us. There is no limit to this. Just as the shepherd does not take a day off from giving his sheep the best, God's restoration is available 24 hours per day.

"He guides me in the paths of righteousness for his name's sake." God our Shepherd knows our spiritual needs as well as our physical ones. In Ezekiel 33:11 He said, "I take no pleasure in the death of the wicked." 2 Peter 3:9 says that God is "not wishing for any to perish but for all to come to repentance." Again picturing an earthly shepherd, we see him guiding his sheep along the safest path. Does that mean there will be no danger along the way? Certainly not, for the predators are lurking in the shadows, ready to attack. But the shepherd is there to guide and guard.

So it is with the Heavenly Shepherd. He wants His sheep to be with Him in eternity. He knows that along the path to the next world, His sheep will face dangers as the "adversary, the devil, prowls around like a roaring lion, seeking someone to devour" (1 Peter 5:8). Still, through the comfort of His Word (1 Thessalonians 4:18) and the commands therein (John 14:15; 15:14; 1 John 5:3), He leads His sheep to the place of eternal rest.

Now the Psalmist shifts from speaking about the Shepherd to speaking to the Shepherd and honoring Him for the tender care that was highlighted in the first three verses. Verses four through six express a calm assurance in God's guidance. There is not a hint of doubt to be found here. The inspired writer has experienced the goodness of God and is confident that He will be with him throughout life and even into the valley of the shadow of death. He has found that the Lord was with him in good times and even in the bad times when the enemy encompassed him. He is certain that the Lord will continue to provide what he needs. In short, he knows this Shepherd, and his knowledge of Him leads to the exultant conclusion in verse six, "Surely goodness and lovingkindness will follow me all the days of my life, and I will dwell in the house of the Lord forever."

Application

God blesses all of mankind. Jesus said, "He causes his sun to rise on the evil and the good, and sends rain on the righteous and the unrighteous" (Matthew 5:45). Any and all blessings enjoyed by humanity come from God above (James 1:17). Unfortunately, not everyone in the world understands this. Many ignore the source of their blessings and thus, when trials come upon them, they think they have no one to whom they can turn. Faithful children of God on the other hand know the source of their blessings. They regularly acknowledge God's provision in their daily service to Him. When they face life's trials, they know where to turn for comfort because they have learned to rely on and trust in God. They know that the One who has sustained them in life's noonday will carry them through the darkest midnight. Like the sheep portrayed in this Psalm, they have seen that the goodness of God endures continually

(Psalm 52:1). They know the Shepherd and confidently look ahead, assured that this Shepherd will be there for them.

The Shepherd knows me and I know the Shepherd. These two facts, that are clearly demonstrated in the twenty-third Psalm, combine to comfort our souls at a depth that no worldly thought could ever fathom. God knows me whether or not I acknowledge Him (Romans 3:3-4). What a joy it is to realize through faith that God knows me well. He understands my every need. He provides what is best for me in whatever situation I may find myself as a faithful Christian. Having this blessed assurance, I can rejoice with the author of this Psalm and confidently apply his Divinely inspired words to my own life no matter how dark or discouraging my way might become.

Key Takeaways from Chapter 4

- God willingly provides His sheep with all that they need.
- God gives His best to His sheep.
- God is always nearby, even as we walk into the valley of the shadow of death.

Moments of Meditation

1. List at least 5 blessings that you have from God. You can write more on a separate piece of paper if you like.

_____

_____

_____

_____

_____

2. What did the Psalmist mean when he wrote that the Shepherd "restores my soul?"

_____

_____

_____

_____

3. What are some examples of God's goodness and lovingkindness in your life?

_____

_____

_____

_____

4. When we are experiencing the grief that comes from a loss, what do we need to do to see the good that is still in our lives?

_____

_____

_____

_____

5. Why is it comforting to realize that God knows you?

_____

_____

_____

_____

_____

Be patient with yourself. You don't want to spend the rest of your life grieving, but you also don't want to put pressure on yourself to "finish grieving" by a certain date.

Chapter Five
Psalm 29
The Comfort of Knowing
that God Is in Control

1 Ascribe to the LORD, O sons of the mighty, ascribe to the LORD glory and strength.

2 Ascribe to the LORD the glory due to His name; worship the LORD in holy array.

3 The voice of the LORD is upon the waters; the God of glory thunders, the LORD is over many waters.

4 The voice of the LORD is powerful, the voice of the LORD is majestic.

5 The voice of the LORD breaks the cedars; yes, the LORD breaks in pieces the cedars of Lebanon.

6 He makes Lebanon skip like a calf, and Sirion like a young wild ox.

7 The voice of the LORD hews out flames of fire.

8 The voice of the LORD shakes the wilderness; the LORD shakes the wilderness of Kadesh.

9 The voice of the LORD makes the deer to calve and strips the forests bare; and in His temple everything says, "Glory!"

10 The LORD sat *as King* at the flood; yes, the LORD sits as King forever.

11 The LORD will give strength to His people; the LORD will bless His people with peace.

Examination of the Psalm

This psalm doesn't require a great deal of explanation. We can break it down into three parts.

- Verses 1-2: Give praise and honor to God.

- Verses 3-10 – Give this praise and honor to Him because He is worthy of it. He is in control of His creation. As the "King forever," He is also in control of eternity.

- Verse 11 – God will give strength and peace to those who honor Him.

God is in control. Nature itself declares this truth as is seen in the references to God's presence in the thunder, the animal kingdom, and the seas. His involvement in the affairs of mankind is evident in verse 11. He is the one who blesses with strength and peace.

Application

One might wonder, "If God is in control, why is there so much suffering in the world? Why doesn't God do something about it?" Even though that's not the subject of this book, allow me to take a moment or two to answer those questions.

The answer lies in the fact that God has given mankind freedom of choice. Now, that may sound like a simplistic solution to some, but it's true. In the Garden of Eden, the first man and woman were given the freedom to choose to obey or not to obey God. In making the wrong choice, they introduced sin into the world (Genesis 3). That creation that had been "very good" (Genesis 1:31) had become corrupt. Now it was subject to wearing down (Psalm 102:25-26). Aging, decay, and ultimately, death, would now result. The imperfections in the world are the result of mankind's fall, not God's lack of power, and we suffer as a result of these imperfections.

On a more personal note, sometimes we suffer as individuals because of poor choices that we make. Our health, our financial situation, our relationships may cause us pain because we have exercised our freedom of choice and have made the wrong decisions. The apostle Paul wrote, "The sins of some men are quite evident, going before them to judgment; for others, their sins follow after" (1 Timothy 5:24).

Sometimes we suffer as individuals because of poor choices that others make. We may suffer from an accident caused by a drunk driver, go through financial difficulties because the company for which we worked closed due to the dishonesty of the owner, or even feel grief over losing a loved one who has made a poor choice.

Again, although the fact that freedom of choice explains the existence of suffering in the world, some don't want to accept this. They feel that God has abandoned them in their sorrow. If they would think about it, they would see that they have put themselves in a difficult position. They want their freedom to do as they please, but then they want God to take away that freedom and intervene so that they won't have to suffer any pain. When Job was encouraged by his wife to curse God and die due to his affliction, he replied, "Shall we indeed accept good from God and not accept adversity?" (Job 2:10). Of course, Job was not charging God with committing wickedness for there is no evil in God (James 1:13). What he was saying is that it's inconsistent to follow God when things are going well and then turn on Him when times get tough. We appreciate the freedom that God has given us when it brings blessings, but do we complain when this same freedom brings difficulties?

Acceptance of the fact that we live in a sinful, imperfect world where tragedies occur and bad things happen to good people is certainly one of the key results of faith. Psalm 29 is so powerful because, coming from the source of our faith (Romans 10:17), it reminds us that no matter how difficult our situation might be, God is aware and in control of that situation.

Now let's get back to the fact that God is in control. By reminding us of this truth, our faith looks beyond this world and its imperfection and into eternity where heaven awaits with its absence of tears, death, sorrow, and pain (Revelation 21:4). Paul painted this beautiful contrast in 1 Corinthians 15:21-22: "For since by a man came death, by a man also came the resurrection of the dead. For as in Adam all die, so also in Christ all will be made alive."

Yes, God is in control. He is not controlling in the sense that He dangles us from a string as a puppeteer does his puppets. He is not dominating our every move, restraining or permitting our actions as though we had no minds of our own. He is in control in the sense that He knows what's going on. He sees us. He hears the prayers of the faithful (Revelation 5:8). Best of all, He has made provision for us to be in a better land than this through obedience to the Gospel that He established through Jesus Christ. He was in control of that opportunity for salvation at least as far back as the Garden of Eden, right after the man and woman wrongly exercised their freedom of choice and sinned (Genesis 3:15).

God is in control. We can look all around us and see the evidence as the Psalmist did. This is especially significant when we face difficulties and feel that our lives are out of control. The truth is, there are indeed times when we cannot be in control. Sometimes, there is only so much that we can do to affect our situation. It's unfortunate that it can take times like this to drive us to our knees and turn to the One who is in control, but, then again, these times of trial can actually benefit us by preparing us for greater service here and eternal rest after this life is over.

In the midst of life's challenges, we must listen to the "voice of the Lord." No, we're not to sit around and wait for the Lord to audibly address us. The voice of the Lord in Psalm 29 was not the literal voice of God. The writer used the term to represent the power and omnipresence of God. Carefully read through the Psalm again, recognizing the greatness of our God, and then pause to realize that this God knows of the difficulties we face when we are in the very midst of them and that He will care for us. He is in the midst of these situations with us. "The Lord will give strength to His people; the Lord will bless His people with peace." He has it all under control.

Key Takeaways from Chapter 5

- God is in control of His creation and of eternity.
- God is aware of what is happening in our lives.
- God has the power to bless us with strength and peace.

Moments of Meditation

1. What do we mean when we say that God is in control?

    _____

    _____

    _____

    _____

    _____

2. What, if anything, is going on in your life right now that you need
    to turn over to God because it's out of your control?

    _____

    _____

    _____

    _____

3. How would you benefit from turning that matter over to God?

    _____

    _____

    _____

    _____

4. How does it comfort you to know that God is aware of all that is going on in your life?

_____

_____

_____

_____

_____

5. Name some areas in your life that you can control (for example, your tongue, your attitude).

_____

_____

_____

_____

_____

In the early stages of your loss, you will be devoting a great deal of attention to your own needs. As you begin your recovery from loss and grief, consider how you might be able to help others who have experienced a loss like yours. Looking outward can make you feel more useful. It can also give you a sense of purpose. Your story of loss, grief, and recovery can be of tremendous help to others.

Chapter Six
Psalm 46
The Comfort of not Being Afraid

[1] God is our refuge and strength, a very present help in trouble.
[2] Therefore we will not fear, though the earth should change and though the mountains slip into the heart of the sea;
[3] Though its waters roar and foam, though the mountains quake at its swelling pride. Selah.
[4] There is a river whose streams make glad the city of God, the holy dwelling places of the Most High.
[5] God is in the midst of her, she will not be moved; God will help her when morning dawns.
[6] The nations made an uproar, the kingdoms tottered; He raised His voice, the earth melted.
[7] The Lord of hosts is with us; the God of Jacob is our stronghold. Selah.
[8] Come, behold the works of the Lord, who has wrought desolations in the earth.
[9] He makes wars to cease to the end of the earth; He breaks the bow and cuts the spear in two; He burns the chariots with fire.
[10] Cease striving and know that I am God; I will be exalted among the nations, I will be exalted in the earth.
[11] The Lord of hosts is with us; the God of Jacob is our stronghold. Selah.

Examination of the Psalm

This psalm opens with a powerful statement regarding God's care. Verse one calls Him our refuge and strength. In this context, a refuge is a shelter from danger. We often need a refuge, a place of protection from the storms of life. Because of His strength, God is able to provide that refuge. Furthermore, God is "very present," meaning that He is always near and readily available when His people are in trouble.

Verses 2-3 indicate that there was trouble in the land when this Psalm was written. We're not told exactly what it was, but the bottom line is that there was no reason to be afraid. God had provided a shelter so that His people could find comfort and peace.

In verses 4-5, God promised to give relief from the turmoil described in the two previous verses. He also promised to provide that relief "when morning dawns." He wasn't going to give His relief grudgingly. He was willing and ready to give it as soon as it was needed.

The psalm continues to allay fear with the reminder that God is near (verses 7 and 11). Fear is further dispelled in verses 6 and 8-9 where God emphasizes that He is aware of what's causing the trouble. Even if His people did not understand what was happening in their lives, God understood.

The grand climax of Psalm 46 is seen in verse 10. With troubles and turmoil swirling all around, God said, "Cease striving and know that I am God." In other words, calm down, stop being afraid, and let thoughts of God and His protection dominate your mind. Stop relying on yourself to have all of the answers. Turn to God and let Him help.

Application

Walking hand in hand with loss and grief, maybe even leading the way for them, is the feeling of fear. When financial challenges arise, fear of loss, fear of failure, and fear of embarrassment or shame tend to rise up. When illness invades our lives, fear of pain, fear of financial distress, and even fear of death make themselves known. When a loved one dies, fear of loneliness can creep in. Each one of these fears is potentially crippling to one's emotional state, one's physical condition and one's spirituality. The fear of God which recognizes the power of the Almighty to relieve these fears is the only way to defeat them.

It's terrible to be afraid, but when we break down fear, we find that it often stems from a lack of knowledge. We're facing trouble and we don't know how it will all turn out. As a result, we're afraid. We've seen horrible things happen to others in situations like ours and we assume that our situation is going to turn out the same way. This family lost their house. That person suffered a lot of pain and spent weeks in the hospital. Often, we've made up our minds that our results will be the same or even worse. Adding to this are the "friends" who seem to take delight in sharing their horror stories with us.

This lack of knowledge, which breeds fear, can easily be replaced with that which conquers fear. God has given us His inspired Word to fill that knowledge gap. Furthermore, He allows us to come and speak to Him in prayer and cast these fears upon Him. Thus, faith replaces fear. There is not enough room in the human heart for both.

In order to gain freedom from fear, we must first acknowledge its presence and then identify it. In verses 2-3, the Psalmist admitted the existence of fear brought about by the potential for troubles. After acknowledging fear, we have to identify it so that we can face it and defeat it.

The unknowns of a loss can produce fear. We can help identify our fears and find the solutions to them by talking openly about them. During the illness of my wife, Shannon, she and I discussed our fears in the early days of her disease. We would ask, "What is making you afraid and why does that scare you?" We shared a fear of the unknown. She feared the cancer treatments, the sickness that might come with them, the loss of hair, and the loss of strength. My fears included those of not being able to adequately take care of her and, of course, that of losing her. As we examined each fear we kept coming back to one conclusion. Whatever we didn't know about what would happen, we were certain that God knew. Whatever fears we entertained were eliminated by such powerful statements as, "I can do all things through Him who strengthens me" (Philippians 4:13). That's how we made it through that particular trial of life. She showed such tremendous courage throughout her ordeal. Even in death she refused to allow fear to discourage her. Faith, grounded firmly in the fear of the Lord, produced fearlessness that allowed her to overcome.

When troubles come and you're afraid, try to determine the source of your fear. Spend time in prayer to God and tell Him what is making you afraid. Psalm 34:18 says that the Lord is nearby. 2 Timothy 1:7 says,

"For God has not given us a spirit of timidity, but of power and love and discipline." 1 John 4:18 reads, "There is no fear in love; but perfect love casts out fear, because fear involves punishment, and the one who fears is not perfected in love." The word for "fear" in this verse means "dread," or "terror." Face the troubling fears and then turn in reverential fear to the One who can deliver you from them.

Key Takeaways from Chapter 6

- God offers refuge from the storms of life.
- God is ready and able to help His people.
- Faith conquers fear.

Moments of Meditation

1. What is your most troubling fear at this time?

_____

_____

_____

_____

_____

2. Why is this particular fear so troubling to you?

_____

_____

_____

_____

3. In what ways is that fear hurting you and hindering your recovery from loss and grief?

_____

_____

_____

_____

_____

4. What can you do to overcome that fear?

_____

_____

_____

_____

_____

5. What is the meaning of, "I can do all things through Him who strengthens me" (Philippians 4:13)?

_____

_____

_____

_____

_____

QUICK TIP

Pay close attention to your self-talk. Are you blaming yourself for your loss even though it wasn't your fault? Are you doubting your ability to move forward from your loss? Replace negative thoughts with positive ones. Philippians 4:8 is a good place to start. There you will find a list of positive things on which to focus. Look at each one, meditate on the meanings, and, if you're able, memorize the verse. If memorization proves difficult, consider writing the verse on a piece of paper and carrying it with you.

Chapter Seven
Psalm 73
The Comfort of God's Patience

[1] Surely God is good to Israel, to those who are pure in heart!

[2] But as for me, my feet came close to stumbling, my steps had almost slipped.

[3] For I was envious of the arrogant as I saw the prosperity of the wicked.

[4] For there are no pains in their death, and their body is fat.

[5] They are not in trouble as *other* men, nor are they plagued like mankind.

[6] Therefore pride is their necklace; the garment of violence covers them.

[7] Their eye bulges from fatness; the imaginations of *their* heart run riot.

[8] They mock and wickedly speak of oppression; they speak from on high.

[9] They have set their mouth against the heavens, and their tongue parades through the earth.

[10] Therefore his people return to this place, and waters of abundance are drunk by them.

[11] They say, "How does God know? And is there knowledge with the Most High?"

[12] Behold, these are the wicked; and always at ease, they have increased *in* wealth.

[13] Surely in vain I have kept my heart pure and washed my hands in innocence;

[14] For I have been stricken all day long and chastened every morning.

[15] If I had said, "I will speak thus," behold, I would have betrayed the generation of Your children.

[16] When I pondered to understand this, it was troublesome in my sight

¹⁷ Until I came into the sanctuary of God; *then* I perceived their end.

¹⁸ Surely You set them in slippery places; You cast them down to destruction.

¹⁹ How they are destroyed in a moment! They are utterly swept away by sudden terrors!

²⁰ Like a dream when one awakes, O Lord, when aroused, You will despise their form.

²¹ When my heart was embittered and I was pierced within,

²² Then I was senseless and ignorant; I was *like* a beast before You.

²³ Nevertheless I am continually with You; You have taken hold of my right hand.

²⁴ With Your counsel You will guide me, and afterward receive me to glory.

²⁵ Whom have I in heaven *but You*? and besides You, I desire nothing on earth.

²⁶ My flesh and my heart may fail, but God is the strength of my heart and my portion forever.

²⁷ For, behold, those who are far from You will perish; You have destroyed all those who are unfaithful to You.

²⁸ But as for me, the nearness of God is my good; I have made the Lord God my refuge, that I may tell of all Your works.

Examination of the Psalm

This Psalm is unique in that the writer states his conclusion in his introduction. He concluded that God is good to those of a clean heart. He does recall a time, however, in which he had forgotten this truth. We could aptly title verses two through fourteen, "Where Was God?" for the writer's words describe a period in his life when he felt that God had withdrawn Himself from the world and forsaken His people.

As has typically been the case throughout history, the society in which this writer lived was filled with wickedness. The evil of those surrounding the Psalmist was compounded by their attitude that either God didn't know about their sinfulness or else didn't care. Their arrogance influenced the Psalmist to question his own service to God. "Surely in vain I have kept my heart pure and washed my hands in innocence." Surely faithfulness was a waste of time. Either God was too weak to act or just wholly unconcerned about both the wicked and the righteous. This is the frame of mind in which the writer found himself. As he had said in verse 2, "But as for me, my feet came close to stumbling, my steps had almost slipped."

When the Psalmist turned his attention from the world and turned his eyes toward God, he saw the truth. He saw that while the wicked may prosper in this life, they will be cast down in eternity. He saw how the scales of prosperity may appear to be tipped toward a life of disobedience while on earth but then realized that the rewards of eternity are far greater than anything this world might have to offer. He repented. He turned back to God. He expressed shame for his foolishness and ignorance.

Application

What does the Psalmist's situation have to do with finding comfort when we're facing loss and grief? Very simply, he wondered about God's care just like we might do in our struggles. "Where was God?" is a typical question on the hearts if not on the lips of those who suffer. "Where was God when my spouse died?" "Where was God when my child was maimed in a car wreck?" "Where was God (fill in the blank)?" The temptation is to conclude that either He doesn't care or, if He does care, perhaps He is too weak to do anything to help. Perhaps there is no hope. Perhaps we've either been abandoned or the One in whom we have put so much trust just can't deliver on the promises that He has made.

Other chapters in this book address how to overcome this doubt. Suffice it to say here that it can be overcome. This chapter is about an underlying theme of Psalm 73. The writer wondered. He questioned. He doubted. In spite of all of this, God was patient with him. The Psalmist wasn't struck dead after writing the last letter of verse 14. God was patient with him.

Wondering about God's care is not uncommon in the Psalms. Psalm 10:1 reads, "Why do you stand afar off, O Lord? Why do you hide

51

yourself in times of trouble?" Psalm 74 begins, "O God, why have you rejected us forever? Why does your anger smoke against the sheep of Your pasture?" Psalm 79 opens with the writer describing the affliction that Jerusalem was enduring at the hands of the heathen. He could not understand why God had not yet intervened (Psalm 79:5). Certainly, we can relate to the frustration of these writers. Perhaps we can even sense an aggravation with God's timing. These writers are neither the first nor the last to want things to happen on their schedule rather than on God's. In spite of their bewilderment and outright questioning of the Lord's ways, they were treated with patience by the benevolent God who created them.

It's interesting to listen to people's observations about incidents recorded in the Bible. Some will read the complaints of Israel in the wilderness after they were freed from Egyptian captivity (Exodus 15ff) and sneer, figuring that these people should have known better. Some will look at the often-seen faithlessness of even the apostles as they walked with Jesus when He was in the flesh and smugly shake their heads in disgust over the weakness of those men who had been hand-picked by Jesus. Thankfully, none of us has been charged with filling God's role. While we might look down our noses at the recorded demonstrations of weak faith, God, who was there when each event occurred, showed patience and allowed for growth like He does when we demonstrate weakness in our faith.

One word that is translated "patience" in the New Testament is a compound word in the original Greek text. It's found in Romans 9:22, 1 Timothy 1:16, 1 Peter 3:20, and 2 Peter 3:15. The first half is the word from which we derive our English word, "macro," meaning large in scale, scope, or capability. The second half has to do with heat, anger or passion. In this compound word, we see our God as one who is great in withholding His anger. He does not respond in the heat of a moment. A variation on this word is found in the Greek text in 2 Peter 3:9 and is translated into English as "patient." "The Lord is not slow about His promise, as some count slowness, but is patient toward you, not wishing for any to perish but for all to come to repentance." Regarding God's response to Israel's complaints and unfaithfulness in the wilderness the Psalmist wrote,

> But He, being compassionate, forgave their iniquity and did not destroy them; and often He restrained His anger and did not arouse all His wrath. Thus, He remembered that they were but flesh, a wind that passes and does not return. (Psalm 78:38-39)

In the throes of Judah's sorrows, Jeremiah wrote, "The Lord's lovingkindnesses indeed never cease, for His compassions never fail. They are new every morning; great is Your faithfulness" (Lamentations 3:22-23). God is patient with the frailties of His creation.

As was mentioned in another chapter, when dealing with life's challenges, we typically talk about the need for time to work through them. It's because our situation is so new, so unfamiliar that we need some time to adjust. In the death of a loved one, for instance, that first night of not having him or her around or that first time that you want to talk to him or her but cannot are scenarios that require adjustment. We have to get used to this uncharted territory in our lives. Some choose to get angry over these unwanted and sometimes unexpected changes. Some question God's goodness and even challenge Him. Thanks be to God that He knows the hearts of those who feel these very real, very human emotional pangs.

Of the many wonderful attributes of our God, one is that He never turns His ear away from any of the prayers of the righteous (1 John 5:14-15). We are invited to cast our cares (anxieties) upon Him (1 Peter 5:7). We can tell Him anything, expressing the deepest feelings from the most remote chambers of our hearts. We can speak to God openly as Habakkuk did in his dilemma (Habakkuk 1:2ff). We can tell Him of our confusion regarding our situation as the writer of Psalm 73 did. Our God understands and we go to Him through our mediator, Jesus Christ (1 Timothy 2:5) who Himself walked in our shoes, as it were, and "has been tempted in all things like we are" (Hebrews 4:15). In fact, because of Christ, we can "draw near with confidence to the throne of grace, so that we may receive mercy and find grace to help in time of need" (Hebrews 4:16). God allows us and even encourages us to pour out our hearts to Him. "Trust in Him at all times, O people; pour out your heart before Him; God is a refuge for us" (Psalm 62:8). He listens patiently, making allowance for our human imperfection. "Just as a father has compassion on his children, so the Lord has compassion on those who fear Him. For He Himself knows our frame; he is mindful that we are but dust" (Psalm 103:13-14).

The Lord inspired the writer of Psalm 73 to put down in words the feelings that had filled his heart in a desperate period of his life. In so doing, God showed that He is aware of His people's lack of understanding and even our doubt when we are afflicted. Of course, it should be pointed out that God's patience can be exhausted. While He showed an incredible measure of longsuffering to Israel in the wilderness, eventually He wearied of the rebellious attitudes and refused to allow many of the Israelites to enter into the promised land of Canaan (Numbers 14). The apostle Paul wrote that God "has fixed a day in which He will judge the world in righteousness through a Man whom He has appointed..." (Acts 17:31). He also wrote that the Lord will exact punishment against those who "do not know God and to those who do not obey the gospel of our Lord Jesus Christ" (2 Thessalonians 1:7-9). Even Christians can go away from God and lose their souls (2 Peter 2:20-22). We must not allow our questioning to turn into disbelief. Instead, we must imitate this Psalmist. Even though at one point he wondered about God's care for him, he nonetheless relied on the faith that he had built through God's Word and ultimately concluded that God is good. If we do like him, we will see that God is caring for us as much in our challenges as He does in our times of peace. May we say with Habakkuk,

> Though the fig tree should not blossom and there be no fruit on the vines, though the yield of the olive should fail and the fields produce no food, though the flock should be cut off from the fold and there be no cattle in the stalls, yet I will exult in the Lord, I will rejoice in the God of my salvation" (Habakkuk 3:17-18).

Let us be thankful that we serve the God who makes a way for us to escape our troubles (1 Corinthians 10:13) and who patiently allows us time to work through them.

Key Takeaways from Chapter 7

- The Psalmists often expressed their concerns to God about His care for them.
- God recognizes that we are weak.
- God allows us to speak openly to Him.

Moments of Meditation

1. What, if anything, are you questioning God about at this time?

_____

_____

_____

_____

_____

2. Why is that matter causing you to question God?

_____

_____

_____

_____

_____

3. Have you talked to God in prayer about it? If not, why not?

_____

_____

_____

_____

_____

4. In what ways has God demonstrated His patience toward you?

_____

_____

_____

_____

_____

5. Why is it comforting to know that we can tell everything to God?

_____

_____

_____

_____

QUICK TIP

Be aware of how much time you spend online. In a time of loss and grief, it's easy to pull away from personal contact with others. While there's nothing wrong with being online in and of itself, face-to-face relationships are the best.

Chapter Eight
Psalm 77
The Comfort of Remembering

[1] My voice rises to God, and I will cry aloud; my voice rises to God, and He will hear me.

[2] In the day of my trouble I sought the Lord; in the night my hand was stretched out without weariness; my soul refused to be comforted.

[3] *When* I remember God, then I am disturbed; *when* I sigh, then my spirit grows faint. *Selah.*

[4] You have held my eyelids *open*; I am so troubled that I cannot speak.

[5] I have considered the days of old, the years of long ago.

[6] I will remember my song in the night; I will meditate with my heart, and my spirit ponders:

[7] Will the Lord reject forever? And will He never be favorable again?

[8] Has His lovingkindness ceased forever? Has His promise come to an end forever?

[9] Has God forgotten to be gracious, or has He in anger withdrawn His compassion? *Selah.*

[10] Then I said, "It is my grief, that the right hand of the Most High has changed."

[11] I shall remember the deeds of the LORD; surely I will remember Your wonders of old.

[12] I will meditate on all Your work and muse on Your deeds.

[13] Your way, O God, is holy; what god is great like our God?

[14] You are the God who works wonders; You have made known Your strength among the peoples.

[15] You have by Your power redeemed Your people, the sons of Jacob and Joseph. *Selah.*

[16] The waters saw You, O God; the waters saw You, they were in anguish; the deeps also trembled.

¹⁷ The clouds poured out water; the skies gave forth a sound; Your arrows flashed here and there.

¹⁸ The sound of Your thunder was in the whirlwind; the lightnings lit up the world; the earth trembled and shook.

¹⁹ Your way was in the sea and Your paths in the mighty waters, and Your footprints may not be known.

²⁰ You led Your people like a flock by the hand of Moses and Aaron.

Examination of the Psalm

The agony being suffered by this Psalmist is clearly seen in the first four verses. His sorrow was so deep that silent prayer was not sufficient to express it. He audibly cried out to God, even through the night. The overwhelming nature of his sadness had robbed him of sleep. It was an anguish that knew no limits, as it spiraled downward from that which could only be expressed out loud to that which was so intense that no words could even come forth from the Psalmist's lips to articulate it.

The setting of this Psalm is open to discussion. It appears to be a captivity Psalm, one written after the citizens of Judah were taken away from their home country into servitude in the land of the Babylonians (2 Chronicles 36:14-21). In verses 7-9, the writer is obviously lamenting a tragic loss. In the final eleven verses, he is bringing to mind a previous deliverance that his ancestors had enjoyed – the deliverance of Israel from Egyptian bondage (Exodus 12-14). In remembering how God had freed Israel from slavery in the past, perhaps the Psalmist is expressing that same hope of God's deliverance of Judah from their present distress.

Look at the contrast of thought in verses 1-9. Initially, the Psalmist writes of how he turned to God in his sorrow, but then he wonders where God is and why He will not answer his earlier pleas. "I begged for relief to the extent that I had no more words to speak. Why has God not answered me? Has He forgotten how to be gracious?" Questioning if God had forgotten is ironic because it is actually the Psalmist himself who had forgotten something. He had forgotten the history of God's goodness toward His people.

Notice how his attitude changes when he says in verse 11, "I shall remember the deeds of the Lord; surely I will remember Your wonders of old." In the Psalmist's despair, he put a halt to the doubts he was having long enough to take time to focus on God (verses 12-13). He meditated on God's works, talked of His doings, and considered His way. In so doing, he recalled that the Lord is "the God who works wonders" (verse 14).

From that point on, he recounts how God had released Israel from the life-stealing grip of the Egyptians. He knew from that historical event that God both could and would do whatever was necessary to aid His people. The amazing power of God is so beautifully portrayed in the Psalmist's statement about the parting of the Red Sea in verse 16: "The waters saw You, O God; the waters saw You, they were in anguish; the deeps also trembled." In verses 18 through 20 he declares that God was to be found everywhere in this scene of deliverance. He was in the thunder and lightning and the quaking of the earth. He was in the midst of the sea. Yet, for all of the demonstration of His might, God carefully led each Israelite through the sea like a shepherd leads his flock.

From distress to doubt to adoration, the Psalmist runs the gamut of emotions, concluding the psalm with his remembrance of God's goodness. He had come to realize that the God who could deliver Israel from Egyptian captivity could certainly answer his pleas and provide the comfort he was so desperately seeking.

Application

The apparent conflict in the heart of the Psalmist is not at all unfamiliar to anyone who has ever been in sorrow. He had forgotten God's care in previous days. We ourselves may pray and plead, hoping, perhaps even expecting, that God will answer our prayers our way, in our time. If He does not, we may begin to question His goodness. We may feel that the distress will never go away. We forget that God has not changed, and perhaps we even forget all the good that we have enjoyed in life at His hand of mercy.

With so many emotions flying around in our heads during times of trouble, it's easy to see how remembrances of God's goodness could be crowded out. That's why it is critical, for the sake of our souls, to stop, take some time for ourselves, and remember. That's what the Psalmist did.

Simply telling someone who has suffered loss and grief, to "remember God" may seem trite and may even be met with anger by the one who is suffering. Some may think I'm being simplistic and even trivializing one's sadness by saying, "Remember God." It may sound like I'm impatiently telling the sorrowful, "Come on; snap out of it. Stop moping around and get over it." Nothing could be further from the truth.

When a loved one dies, what is one of the first things done by those left behind? Certainly, we cry and hurt and maybe even question, but do we not also remember? Most likely we find ourselves sitting around a dinner table with family and friends sharing pleasant memories of the deceased. There is great comfort in this. As weeks, months, and years pass, we will still remember different things about our beloved. Memories might be triggered by a scent, a picture, a song, or even a phrase.

If remembering moments in the lives of our departed loved ones can cheer us and bring us comfort, why wouldn't remembering God's goodness bring us even greater joy and peace? If we can sit around and begin conversations with, "Remember when he (or she) did this or that" and not get angry or take offense, then why can we not just as well begin conversations with, "Remember when God said this in His Word?" or "Remember when God blessed you with…"? A memory is a valuable tool in so many ways, not the least of which is in bringing to mind the numerous demonstrations of God's goodness both as recorded in His Word and as experienced in our lives.

In whatever situation we may be, we can remember how God blessed His faithful followers in life's daylight, led them through life's midnight, and promised to do the same for us if we are faithful Christians.

- When in financial straits, we can go to Matthew 6:25-34 and remember our value in the eyes of God as well as His promise: "But seek first His kingdom and His righteousness, and all these things will be added to you" (Matthew 6:33).

- When grieving, we can go to the eleventh chapter of John and remember the compassion of Jesus as He wept with the family and friends of Lazarus (John 11:35).

- When lonely, we can consult Hebrews 13:5-6 in which the inspired writer stated, "… for He Himself has said, I will never desert you, nor will I ever forsake you,' so that we may confidently say, The Lord is my Helper, I will not be afraid. What will man do to me?"

- When we feel like giving up, we can turn to Romans 8 and remember Paul's inspired words regarding hope, God's providential care, and the Lord's amazing love.

- When it seems that the pull of the world is too strong, we can go to 1 John 4:4 and remember the words of the apostle John: "You are from God, little children, and have overcome them; because greater is He who is in you than he who is in the world."

- When we ourselves are facing death, we can read the fifteenth chapter of 1 Corinthians regarding the resurrection unto eternal life, especially the final five verses.

But when this perishable will have put on the imperishable, and this mortal will have put on immortality, then will come about the saying that is written, "Death is swallowed up in victory. O death, where is your victory? O death, where is your sting?" The sting of death is sin, and the power of sin is the law; but thanks be to God, who gives us the victory through our Lord Jesus Christ. Therefore, my beloved brethren, be steadfast, immovable, always abounding in the work of the Lord, knowing that your toil is not in vain in the Lord.

Not only can we remember the inspired records of God's help and His promises, but we can also recall in our own lives how greatly God has always blessed us.

In the early stages of a loss, grief is deeply rooted in our hearts. It certainly will not subside overnight and may linger for days or weeks on end. In this context about all we can see and feel is our grief and its cause.

It takes effort, sometimes considerable effort, but there are fond remembrances of God's goodness within us just waiting to come forth and bring us comfort. Remembering these things does not diminish the depth of the sadness, but it can cause us to stop and realize how great God has been to us through the years. In fact, it could remind us that even in our despair, God is still as close as He has ever been. To live in the past is unproductive, but to visit it from time to time through remembering the marvelous blessings of God can make our present more bearable and our future brighter. "Be glad in the Lord, you righteous ones, and give thanks to His holy name." (Psalm 97:12).

Key Takeaways from Chapter 8

- God has been good to every one of us.
- Remembering God's goodness in our past can help us develop trust in His care for us now and in the future.
- Even in our despair, God is still as close as He has ever been.

Moments of Meditation

1. In Hebrews 13:5, God says, "I will never desert you, nor will I ever forsake you." Is that comforting to you? Why is it or why is it not?

_____

_____

_____

_____

_____

2. In this psalm, the writer seems to have been having up and down moments in which he was trusting God in one moment and questioning him in another. Is this something that you have experienced in your time of loss and grief?

_____

_____

_____

_____

_____

3. How will remembering God's blessings in your life help comfort you now?

_____

_____

_____

_____

_____

4. What is your favorite Bible verse that reminds you of God's care for you?

_____

_____

_____

_____

5. Why is that your favorite?

_____

_____

_____

_____

_____

Loss and grief can cloud our minds to the point that we forget God's care for us through the years. Getting together with someone who has known you well for many years can help you see how the Lord has blessed you because they're looking at your life from a different perspective. Think of someone who has known you well for many years. Contact that person and ask him or her to share some memories of how God has blessed you.

Chapter Nine
Psalm 84
Comfort "At the End of the Day"

¹ How lovely are Your dwelling places, O LORD of hosts!

² My soul longed and even yearned for the courts of the Lord; my heart and my flesh sing for joy to the living God.

³ The bird also has found a house, and the swallow a nest for herself, where she may lay her young, even Your altars, O LORD of hosts, my King and my God.

⁴ How blessed are those who dwell in Your house! They are ever praising You. *Selah.*

⁵ How blessed is the man whose strength is in You, in whose heart are the highways *to Zion*!

⁶ Passing through the valley of Baca they make it a spring; the early rain also covers it with blessings.

⁷ They go from strength to strength, *every one of them* appears before God in Zion.

⁸ O LORD God of hosts, hear my prayer; give ear, O God of Jacob! *Selah.*

⁹ Behold our shield, O God, and look upon the face of Your anointed.

¹⁰ For a day in Your courts is better than a thousand *outside.* I would rather stand at the threshold of the house of my God than dwell in the tents of wickedness.

¹¹ For the Lord God is a sun and shield; the LORD gives grace and glory; no good thing does He withhold from those who walk uprightly.

¹² O LORD of hosts, how blessed is the man who trusts in You!

Examination of the Psalm

People like to use the phrase, "at the end of the day." For example, a nurse might say something like, "Well, yes, the work I do is difficult, but at the end of the day it's a good feeling to know that I've been able to help someone." When one uses this phrase, he or she is saying that in spite of any apparent drawbacks to their situation or any apparent positives of someone else's situation, they're still thankful to be who they are and where they are.

At the end of the day, this Psalmist was a child of God. Whatever else the world had to offer, whatever challenges life presented, he declared that he would rather be the lowliest servant waiting on others at the door of God's house than have a fine existence away from the Lord and in service to Satan.

The entire psalm paints a beautiful picture of how wonderful it is to be a child of God. There is great joy in serving God (verse 3). Blessings and happiness follow those who abide in the Lord (verses 4- 5). The reason for this happiness is because of God who alone is the sun and shield, the source of grace and glory, the giver of bountiful blessings (verse 11).

"For a day in Your courts is better than a thousand outside." Just one day following God is better than a thousand following Satan. This single day, though it be filled with the world's snares, is worth more than a thousand days of temporal pleasure lived in service to the king of the damned. If one day in God's service is worth this much, a lifetime of faithfulness to Him has value beyond compare.

Application

Think about the loss you have suffered and the grief you are feeling. Is it possible that those who don't obey God are free from these troubles? Would you be better off to give up on God and just fall in with the world so that your problems will go away? The answer is a resounding "NO"! Those who live in disobedience to God have troubles too. They get sick, lose loved ones, and have personal struggles just like faithful Christians do. BUT AT THE END OF THE DAY, it's the Christian who has the Lord as his or her sun and shield, it's the Christian who has an eternal shoulder on which to lean and a loving ear ready to hear (1 Peter 5:7; Revelation 5:8), and it's the Christian who has the hope of eternal rest when this life is over (Romans 8:24-25).

Satan delights in seeing trouble come upon the human race. His ultimate desire is to have as many as he can with him in eternal hell (1 Peter 5:8). To him, troubles serve as a way to retrieve those who turned to God and a way to hang on to those who are currently serving him.

Psalm 84 shows us that Satan really has nothing worthwhile to offer us. When we turn our backs on God as a result of loss and grief, we turn to one who is inferior to God in every way and who, at best, offers us only temporary relief, if it can even be called relief. The "relief" that an ungodly life offers to our loss and grief is found in drugs, indecent living, anger, and bitterness. On the other hand, when our hearts and flesh cry out for the living God (verse 2), we find blessings, grace, and peace, as well as the strength we need to endure (verses 4-5).

It may seem sometimes that we are fighting a losing battle, that the pain that befalls us is too great to bear, and that it's just not worth the daily effort to follow God faithfully. This Psalm proves otherwise. People of the world may boast of their lives, but at the end of the day, it's the faithful child of God who has the comfort and strength that he or she needs to handle life's issues. Following God faithfully, even in the midst of struggles, is never a mistake, but is always rewarding.

The phrase, "the end of the day" brings to mind the story of the cross-bearing man who walked into the "cross store." He laid down his cross and said to the proprietor, "I want a lighter cross please; one that's easier to carry." The proprietor invited him to look around the store. The shopper went from one cross to another, examining each carefully. He tried to lift one but was barely able to budge it. Just glancing at another, he knew that he could never handle it. One by one he eliminated those that he figured would be too burdensome. Finally, he came to one that looked manageable. He picked it up and marveled at how light it was. "I'll take this one," the man said. "That one, sir," answered the proprietor, "is the one you carried in here." So often we think our lot in life is worse than anyone else's, only to discover "at the end of the day" that it's not so unbearable after all.

Key Takeaways from Chapter 9

- The greatest blessing is to be a child of God.
- There is nothing in this world that is worth having if you must quit following God to have it.
- No loss or grief is too much to handle when we are walking faithfully with God.

Moments of Meditation

1. How does serving others help you recover from loss and grief?

    _____

    _____

    _____

    _____

    _____

2. What is the meaning of, "The Lord God is a sun" in verse 11?

    _____

    _____

    _____

    _____

3. What did John mean when he wrote, "greater is He who is in you than he who is in the world" (1 John 4:4)?

    _____

_____

_____

_____

_____

4. At this stage of your grief, do you believe that recovery from it is possible? Why do you or why do you not believe this?

_____

_____

_____

_____

5. What, if anything, can you do differently to help you recover from your loss and grief?

_____

_____

_____

_____

If your grief has been caused by the loss of a loved one, consider keeping their memory alive by donating to their favorite charity in their name, creating a scholarship at their alma mater, or even planting a tree in their name. By doing this, future generations will be able to know that your loved one left a positive impact on the world.

Chapter Ten
Psalm 91
Comfort in Knowing That
Nothing Can Really Harm Us

[1] He who dwells in the shelter of the Most High will abide in the shadow of the Almighty.

[2] I will say to the Lord, "My refuge and my fortress, my God, in whom I trust!"

[3] For it is He who delivers you from the snare of the trapper and from the deadly pestilence.

[4] He will cover you with His pinions, and under His wings you may seek refuge; His faithfulness is a shield and bulwark.

[5] You will not be afraid of the terror by night, or of the arrow that flies by day;

[6] Of the pestilence that stalks in darkness, or of the destruction that lays waste at noon.

[7] A thousand may fall at your side and ten thousand at your right hand, but it shall not approach you.

[8] You will only look on with your eyes and see the recompense of the wicked.

[9] For you have made the LORD, my refuge, even the Most High, your dwelling place.

[10] No evil will befall you, nor will any plague come near your tent.

[11] For He will give His angels charge concerning you, to guard you in all your ways.

[12] They will bear you up in their hands, that you do not strike your foot against a stone.

[13] You will tread upon the lion and cobra, the young lion and the serpent you will trample down.

[14] "Because he has loved Me, therefore I will deliver him; I will set him *securely* on high, because he has known My name.

¹⁵ "He will call upon Me, and I will answer him; I will be with him in trouble; I will rescue him and honor him.
¹⁶ "With a long life I will satisfy him and let him see My salvation."

Examination of the Psalm

This Psalm portrays life's potential crises. A snare, pestilence, terror, an arrow, destruction, people falling by the way, evil, a plague, a lion, and a cobra are the dangers lurking about. Perhaps we would never literally face a lion or arrows, but the troubles we do face can be just as harmful and just as painful in their own ways.

The tremendous truth that stands out in this psalm is that even though these pitfalls line our pathway, none of them can really harm us as long as we walk with God. To be sure, they might set us back, but they cannot conquer us. Faithful followers of God have the Lord as their refuge and fortress. He is the cooling shadow in the noonday heat of Satan's angry attacks. He is like the mother hen who shelters her young from the storm. He is the deliverer and the protector.

Is the Psalmist saying that he would never have any trouble in life? After all, verse ten says, "No evil will befall you." We know that he was not trouble free. If David was the writer, he had family troubles as well as difficulties brought about by foreign enemies and even his own countrymen. If this was written by a Psalmist during the Babylonian captivity, just being held as a prisoner in a foreign land would have been trouble enough.

Is the psalm a guarantee of no problems in life? No. Is it a reassurance that God will keep a watch over His faithful ones when life's difficulties present themselves? Yes. Is it an affirmation that, despite the challenges of this life, God's faithful will ultimately be delivered by the Lord in eternity? Indeed, it is.

Application

As we read this psalm and consider the application of its message, it's easy to think of the apostle Paul and the struggles he faced as a faithful Christian. He spoke of these difficulties twice in his second letter to the Lord's church in the city of Corinth.

In 2 Corinthians 4:8-9, Paul wrote: "We are afflicted in every way, but not crushed; perplexed, but not despairing; persecuted, but not forsaken; struck down, but not destroyed." In Paul's mind, he could be touched by these challenges but not defeated by them. Even though the troubles he faced left visible marks on his body (2 Corinthians 4:10), his perspective on them is clearly seen a few verses later in his statement, "For momentary, light affliction is producing for us an eternal weight of glory far beyond all comparison" (2 Corinthians 4:17).

In 2 Corinthians 11:23-27 Paul penned these words by Divine inspiration:

> Are they servants of Christ? - I speak as if insane - I more so; in far more labors, in far more imprisonments, beaten times without number, often in danger of death. Five times I received from the Jews thirty-nine lashes. Three times I was beaten with rods, once I was stoned, three times I was shipwrecked, a night and a day I have spent in the deep. I have been on frequent journeys, in dangers from rivers, dangers from robbers, dangers from my countrymen, dangers from the Gentiles, dangers in the city, dangers in the wilderness, dangers on the sea, dangers among false brethren; I have been in labor and hardship, through many sleepless nights, in hunger and thirst, often without food, in cold and exposure.

Paul considered none of these difficulties to be of permanent harm. Instead, he saw them as opportunities to glorify God (2 Corinthians 11:30).

As parents, we want our children to have all they need and to be safe. Because of our love for our children, we do all that we can to accomplish these ends in their lives. As our children grow, they begin to make their own decisions. Some are good while others are not so good. As we watch them mature, we give counsel and direction, but we do not so meticulously govern their lives that we rob them of their freedom. We do not keep them from everything that could harm them, but, as loving parents, we are always there for them when troubles come. This well illustrates the points made earlier in this chapter.

Notice verses 11 and 12 of Psalm 91. You might recall how Satan tried to misuse these words in his face-to-face temptation of Jesus.

> Then the devil took Him into the holy city and had Him stand on the pinnacle of the temple, and said to Him, If You are the Son of God, throw Yourself down; for it is written, He will command His angels concerning you; and on their hands they will bear you up, so that You will not strike Your foot against a stone. (Matthew 4:5-6).

Satan's ploy was to persuade Jesus that God would not allow anything harmful to happen to Him. Even if He were to jump from the top of the temple, He would be rescued and would not suffer the slightest bruise, Satan suggested. Jesus knew that this was not the intent of Psalm 91. The Messiah understood that the Psalm was not a guarantee of a trouble-free life. Instead, the Lord showed His confidence in the fact that whatever harm Satan might try to cause, his efforts would have only temporary effects. "Jesus said to him, On the other hand, it is written, You shall not put the Lord your God to the test." (Matthew 4:7). Jesus knew the trouble He would face during His earthly tenure, but He also knew that He would have the victory in His faithful service to the Father.

What harm can life's troubles really do to us? We can allow them to discourage us, make us cry, and become stressed. We can permit them to make us afraid and full of worry. If we allow them to turn us away from God, they can separate us from Him. But as we walk hand in hand with the Lord, we again have to ask, "What can these trials and tribulations really do to us?" If we walk faithfully with the Lord and trust His will, can life's challenges really have any power over us?

Psalm 27:1 reads, "The Lord is my light and my salvation; whom shall I fear? the Lord is the defense of my life; whom shall I dread?" Is there really anything in life that is so discouraging, so stressful, so heart-rending that it can break us? Due to our human frailties, we may bend, but we need not break. Nothing can really harm us if we will trust God and faithfully follow Him.

Key Takeaways from Chapter 10

- God is near when we are in danger.
- God's faithful will ultimately be delivered by the Lord in eternity
- Earth's troubles are temporary.

Moments of Meditation

1. Prior to what you are experiencing now, describe one previous incident of loss and grief.

_____

_____

_____

_____

_____

2. How long ago did that incident happen?

_____

_____

_____

_____

3. Do you feel that you are still recovering from that?

_____

_____

_____

_____

_____

4. What are you doing differently to handle your loss and grief in your current battle?

_____

_____

_____

_____

_____

5. In what ways can life's challenges make us stronger?

_____

_____

_____

_____

_____

Some losses, like losing your job, require a major life change. You'll need a new job, and you might have to move in order to get one that's best for you. Other losses, such as the death of a loved one, should not lead to rash decisions regarding your future. You will want to take your time and make your decisions on where you will go and what you will do based on careful study and sound judgment.

Chapter Eleven
Psalm 93
The Comfort of Knowing that
God Is Bigger than Our Troubles

¹ The LORD reigns, He is clothed with majesty; the LORD has clothed and girded Himself with strength; indeed, the world is firmly established, it will not be moved.

² Your throne is established from of old; You are from everlasting.

³ The floods have lifted up, O LORD, the floods have lifted up their voice, the floods lift up their pounding waves.

⁴ More than the sounds of many waters, than the mighty breakers of the sea, the LORD on high is mighty.

⁵ Your testimonies are fully confirmed; holiness befits Your house, O LORD, forevermore.

Examination of the Psalm

It's clear that this brief Psalm was written to extol the majesty of God. In it we also see at least by implication a marvelous contrast between the majestic God and the rulers of earthly kingdoms.

- God is majestic. He is clothed (fully covered) in majesty as well as strength, as opposed to earthly rulers who are weak by comparison.

- God has always reigned (cf. Psalm 90:1-2), as opposed to the earthly rulers who would come and go.

- God's words are always sure (sound and faithful) while the words of earthly rulers pass away.

- God is the very definition of holiness (1 Peter 1:16), a trait greatly lacking in, if not completely absent from, the lives of the world's leaders.

Continuing his praise for the majesty of God, the Psalmist pays tribute to the Lord's awesome power. To say that God is stronger than literal floods is impressive. Indeed, He is that strong.

The Psalmist wants to demonstrate that God is sovereign, that His majesty exceeds all earthly bounds. To that end, he uses the floods and noise of many waters to represent the troubles facing God's people. In the immediate context, reference is made to those nations who oppressed Israel. "Floods" is used in this manner in other passages (2 Samuel 22:5; Psalm 18:4). "Sounds" is also used in this fashion in Jeremiah 46:17 where the weeping prophet wrote that Pharaoh, king of Egypt, was only a noise, a temporary source of trouble. These figures are not limited to oppression from ungodly kingdoms though. In Psalm 69:2 David wrote in reference to his troubled life in general, "I have sunk in deep mire, and there is no foothold: I have come into deep waters, and a flood overflows me."

There appears to be a progression of danger in these figures. First come the floods, then the waves, then the noise of many waters, then the mighty waves of the sea. The floods are frightening enough, but when the lashing waves and their horrible din are added to the mix, the scene portrayed is one that can lead to fear and distress. Keep in mind, however, that regardless of the power of these noisome waves, the Lord is mightier. Those who have ever seen video of or witnessed a tsunami can readily bring to mind a picture of an overpowering wave. Still, God is greater. He is clothed with majesty. He is bigger than any tempest, be it literally produced by the sea, or figuratively produced in our lives.

Application

Because God is bigger than our troubles, He is quite capable of leading us through them. Not only that, but He is also fully acquainted with any difficulties we might face. Solomon wrote, "That which has been is that which will be, and that which has been done is that which will be done. So there is nothing new under the sun" (Ecclesiastes 1:9).

God has witnessed every storm through which His people have passed. What's more, He has been by their side through every potentially perilous flood of trouble.

- God was with Joseph when he was nearly murdered, sold by his brothers, mistreated by his master, and forgotten by his friend (Genesis 37-50). Joseph was outnumbered and politically overpowered in his difficulties, yet the God who is bigger than our troubles delivered him.

- He was with Hananiah, Mishael, and Azariah when they were cast into the fiery furnace for their faith (Daniel 3). The three Hebrews faced the intimidating heat of a furnace that had been elevated to seven times its normal temperature, a temperature so high that the men who led the three to their intended doom perished in the flame (Daniel 3:19,22). In spite of this, the God who is bigger than our troubles delivered them.

- He stood by the side of Daniel in the lions' den (Daniel 6). Daniel stood face to face with not one, but several lions. How many of those ferocious beasts were in that den is unknown to us, but certainly, confronting even one of them would be frightening beyond words. Nonetheless, the God who is bigger than our troubles delivered Daniel.

We may never physically be in situations like those experienced by Joseph, but emotionally we can feel outnumbered and overpowered by our troubles. We may never physically face the withering heat of a fiery furnace, but in our hearts, we can feel the burn of distress and anguish. We may never physically stand among lions, but the fear and anxiety evoked by our troubles could be just as intense. Despite the enormity of the trials in which we may find ourselves, God is bigger.

There is nothing that burdens us that is too large to take to God. For that matter, there is nothing too small either. The familiar hymn says:

> O what peace we often forfeit,
> O what needless pain we bear,
> All because we do not carry
> Everything to God in prayer.

It's been said that if a thing is too small to take to God in prayer, then it is too small to worry about. If it is big enough to take to God in prayer and we have done that, then we should not worry about it.

When we approach God with our troubles, we are going to the One who is above us.

> For My thoughts are not your thoughts, nor are your ways My ways,' declares the Lord. 'For as the heavens are higher than the earth, so are My ways higher than your ways and My thoughts than your thoughts. (Isaiah 55:8-9).

Our God is bigger than our troubles. What makes this truth even more comforting is the fact that this great God loves us (1 John 4:9), cares for us (1 Peter 5:7) and invites us to cast these burdens upon Him. "Cast your burden upon the Lord and He will sustain you; He will never allow the righteous to be shaken" (Psalm 55:22).

Key Takeaways from Chapter 11

- God is superior in every way to all earthly rulers.
- God is able to help us through all of our troubles, no matter how big they may seem to be.
- God's words are always sound and faithful.

Moments of Meditation

1. Why is knowing that God is bigger than our troubles a comforting thought?

_____

_____

_____

2. How many of our troubles is God able to help us with?

3. Which of our troubles is too little to take to God?

4. How often should we take our troubles to God?

5. Why do we not always take our troubles to God?

_____

_____

_____

_____

_____

If you don't already do so, try saying "thank you" and complimenting others whenever possible. You don't want to come across as insincere, so be sure there is something for which to be thankful and something deserving of a compliment. In doing this, your mind will be focusing on good things that will crowd out the bad things on your mind because of your loss.

Chapter Twelve
Psalm 95
The Comfort of Fellowship in Worship

[1] O come, let us sing for joy to the LORD, let us shout joyfully to the rock of our salvation.

[2] Let us come before His presence with thanksgiving, let us shout joyfully to Him with psalms.

[3] For the LORD is a great God and a great King above all gods,

[4] In whose hand are the depths of the earth, the peaks of the mountains are His also.

[5] The sea is His, for it was He who made it, and His hands formed the dry land.

[6] Come, let us worship and bow down, let us kneel before the LORD our Maker.

[7] For He is our God, and we are the people of His pasture and the sheep of His hand. Today, if you would hear His voice,

[8] Do not harden your hearts, as at Meribah, as in the day of Massah in the wilderness,

[9] "When your fathers tested Me, they tried Me, though they had seen My work.

[10] "For forty years I loathed *that* generation, and said they are a people who err in their heart, and they do not know My ways.

[11] "Therefore I swore in My anger, truly they shall not enter into My rest."

Examination of the Psalm

Israel was invited to come together to worship God. The Lord had shown Himself worthy of praise and adoration. In what better way could the Israelites demonstrate their love and thankfulness to Him than in uniting as one in worship? Surely, they would themselves be strengthened in the faith by banding together with a common focus and a common purpose with their worship being grounded in God's Word.

Their worship was directed to the one true God who was above all of the man-made gods. They were to exalt the One who was their maker and their daily caretaker. Their hearts and minds were to be centered on the great God and King who held their eternity in His hands. What a powerful setting for honoring God and what a tremendous source of strength and comfort for the worshippers.

Application

Worship has always been a vital part of the lives of God's people. We can go back to the Patriarchal age and find faithful servants of God worshipping Him (Genesis 4:4; 12:8; 28:18-22, et al.). They also worshipped Him during the Mosaic period (Exodus 20:1ff; et al.). Today, faithful Christians worship him according to the New Testament pattern (John 4:23-24; Hebrews 10:24-25).

There are many blessings to be found in worshipping God. As it relates to the subject of comfort, one of these blessings is the fact that in worship we turn our attention away from self and toward the Lord. Comfort is hard to find if we focus only on ourselves and our sorrows. Turning to God in worship affords us the opportunity to look upward and set our hearts and minds on the One who can help us handle our troubles and provide the comfort we so desperately desire.

Fellowship is also rich in blessings. There are many "one another" passages in the Bible that show us how much we have to gain in fellowship with those of like precious faith (John 13:34; 15:12,17; Galatians 5:13; 6:2; Ephesians 4:2,32; Colossians 3:13,16; 1 Thessalonians 4:18; 5:11; Hebrews 3:13; 10:24,25; 1 Peter 1:22; 1 John 3:11,23; 4:7,11; 2 John 5). Paul seems to sum it up in this statement in Romans 12:10: "Be devoted to one another in brotherly love; give preference to one another in honor."

The combination of worshipping God and engaging in fellowship with His faithful children has two benefits. It allows us to direct our focus upward. At the same time, we benefit from the participation and encouragement of those around us who themselves are benefiting from their worship of the Lord. In short, gathering for worship is a marvelous tool for helping us handle life's troubles.

In this book, I've tried not to give a lot of personal examples, but I find it necessary here because of how much strength and comfort my wife, Shannon, and I gained from this fellowship during her illness and how much I continue to benefit from it now that she's gone. Worshipping with the saints had long been a regular practice in our home as well as in the homes in which we grew up. Assembling with the church never became trite or boring. These times were opportunities we enjoyed.

How well I remember one particular autumn Sunday. Due to her illness, Shannon had not been able to assemble with the church for worship for several weeks. On this particular Lord's Day, she was well enough to go. As the first hymn began, Shannon and I both joined in with the rest of the congregation. What her professionally trained voice lacked in strength at that moment was made up for with her heart. I looked at her as we sang. She had a huge smile on her face and tears of joy in her eyes as she looked back at me. She was there in worship with the church. The soul-soothing strength it brought her could never be measured.

After Shannon's passing, I found myself, like all who grieve, having my good days and my bad days. I kept a daily journal of what I was feeling. After a couple of months, I went back and read my entries and noticed a pattern. The best days I had in the time immediately following Shannon's death were Sundays and Wednesdays, those days of the week in which the church assembled for worship and Bible classes. The same is true as I write these words today.

The Lord knew there would be tremendous value in Christians worshipping together. That's why He commanded it. The Divinely inspired author of Hebrews wrote, "Let us hold fast the confession of our hope without wavering, for He who promised is faithful; and let us consider how to stimulate one another to love and good deeds, not forsaking our own assembling together, as is the habit of some, but encouraging one another; and all the more as you see the day drawing near" (Hebrews 10:23-25). We know by example that the New Testament church met together for worship every first day of the week (Acts 20:7; I Corinthians 16:1-2). To be able on a regular basis to get away from the world and focus on our wonderful God and to do it with those who love Him and His Word is joyful and peaceful.

Key Takeaways from Chapter 12

- Worshipping God according to His will can be a tremendous source of strength and comfort for the worshippers.
- In worship, we turn our attention away from self and toward the Lord.
- We can receive encouragement from those with whom we worship.

Moments of Meditation

1. In what ways does worshipping God help us recover from our loss and grief?

_____

_____

_____

_____

2. What blessings do we receive from assembling with God's faithful children in worship?

_____

_____

_____

_____

3. Is it wrong to spend time thinking about our needs? Why or why not?

_____

_____

_____

_____

_____

4. Is it wrong to ONLY spend time thinking about our needs? Why or why not?

_____

_____

_____

_____

_____

5. What are some characteristics of God that make Him worthy of our praise?

_____

_____

_____

_____

_____

Address any business matters related to your loss that need your attention. It's difficult to focus on these things while you're grieving, but life is still going on around you even in your time of sadness. There may be bills that need to be paid as well as other financial and legal matters that will need your attention. You might consider hiring a professional in these fields to assist you.

Chapter Thirteen
Psalm 102
Comfort in Prayer

[1] Hear my prayer, O LORD! And let my cry for help come to You.
[2] Do not hide Your face from me in the day of my distress; incline Your ear to me; in the day when I call answer me quickly.
[3] For my days have been consumed in smoke, and my bones have been scorched like a hearth.
[4] My heart has been smitten like grass and has withered away, indeed, I forget to eat my bread.
[5] Because of the loudness of my groaning my bones cling to my flesh.
[6] I resemble a pelican of the wilderness; I have become like an owl of the waste places.
[7] I lie awake, I have become like a lonely bird on a housetop.
[8] My enemies have reproached me all day long; those who deride me have used my *name* as a curse.
[9] For I have eaten ashes like bread and mingled my drink with weeping
[10] Because of Your indignation and Your wrath, for You have lifted me up and cast me away.
[11] My days are like a lengthened shadow, and I wither away like grass.
[12] But You, O LORD, abide forever, and Your name to all generations.
[13] You will arise *and* have compassion on Zion; for it is time to be gracious to her, for the appointed time has come.
[14] Surely Your servants find pleasure in her stones and feel pity for her dust.
[15] So the nations will fear the name of the LORD and all the kings of the earth Your glory.
[16] For the LORD has built up Zion; He has appeared in His glory.
[17] He has regarded the prayer of the destitute and has not despised their prayer.

¹⁸ This will be written for the generation to come, that a people yet to be created may praise the LORD.

¹⁹ For He looked down from His holy height; from heaven the LORD gazed upon the earth,

²⁰ To hear the groaning of the prisoner, to set free those who were doomed to death,

²¹ That men may tell of the name of the LORD in Zion and His praise in Jerusalem,

²² When the peoples are gathered together, and the kingdoms, to serve the LORD.

²³ He has weakened my strength in the way; He has shortened my days.

²⁴ I say, "O my God, do not take me away in the midst of my days, Your years are throughout all generations.

²⁵ "Of old You founded the earth, and the heavens are the work of Your hands.

²⁶ "Even they will perish, but You endure; and all of them will wear out like a garment; like clothing You will change them and they will be changed.

²⁷ "But You are the same, and Your years will not come to an end.

²⁸ "The children of Your servants will continue, and their descendants will be established before You."

Examination of the Psalm

This Psalm is entitled, "A Prayer of the Afflicted, when he is faint and pours out his complaint before the Lord." As was noted in another chapter, while the titles of the psalms are uninspired, they nonetheless provide insight into at least some Bible readers' understanding of the message. That this is a prayer is evident from the first verse. That this is a prayer pouring forth from an afflicted, overwhelmed heart is clear from ensuing verses.

The misery being experienced by this Psalmist is seen in his assessment of his condition. Emotionally, he despairs of life (verse 3), his heart has taken a beating (verse 4), and he is lonely (verse 7). Physically, his anguish is so great that he can neither eat (verse 4) nor sleep (verse 7). His tears are many (verse 9).

If this is a captivity Psalm as some suggest, then the picture here is of one who is missing his homeland and is saddened by the actions that led to his current state. He is discouraged by the apparent power of the enemies of God and perhaps even their arrogance. He looks forward in hope to restoration but in the meantime, he pleads for God's comfort and care.

Throughout the Psalm, there is a marvelous contrast between the brevity of the writer's life and the eternal nature of God. "For my days have been consumed in smoke…" (verse 3). "My days are like a lengthened shadow, and I wither away like grass. But You, O Lord, abide forever, and Your name to all generations" (verses 11-12). Verses 24-27 draw out the contrast between the eternal God and His temporal creation. Verses 25 through 27 are quoted in the New Testament in Hebrews 1:10-12.

There is a beautiful formula in Psalm 102. Take a person in distress, add that person's recognition of his own frailty, then add his realization of God's eternality, and finally add the hope that comes from a heart that trusts in God's care and the end result is fervent prayer.

Application

Who can successfully deny the power of acceptable prayer as a source of comfort for the faithful child of God? Isn't prayer one of the first acts in which we engage when a trial comes upon us? Immediately we pray for relief from and removal of the difficulty. Often, this initial prayer is little more than a silent utterance of "Lord, help me." When we face life's challenges, we know we need to do something in response. Prayer is that response the vast majority of the time.

One of the reasons that prayer brings comfort is because it allows us to speak our minds. In the field of psychiatry this could be termed a catharsis, a "purging of the emotions or relieving of emotional tensions." Of course, perhaps the same could be said for shouting at a wall or standing on the beach and screaming at the ocean at the top of one's lungs. Either of those would provide a release, but neither effort has any definite direction.

In prayer, we can "purge emotions," but faith rooted in the Word of God informs us that we are casting these emotions upon the Lord (1 Peter 5:7). Long-term comfort comes from knowing that God is not only listening to the prayer of the broken-hearted Christian, but He is also answering. James wrote, "The effective prayer of a righteous man can accomplish much" (James 5:16).

For what do Christians pray when in distress? Again, in the early stages of loss and grief, we pray for things to change. We don't want to die, or we don't want a loved one to die, or we don't want to suffer. We want things to change. The apostle Paul wanted his thorn in the flesh to be removed (2 Corinthians 12:8). Numerous prayers are found not only in the Psalms but in other works of inspired writers of the Old Testament where they were pleading for a release from their circumstances.

As we progress through the difficulty, we may still ask for things to change but we may also begin asking for the ability to accept the situation as it is and the ability to handle it more effectively. As Christians, we are concerned about our influence. We are also concerned about staying strong in the faith "so that no advantage would be taken of us by Satan, for we are not ignorant of his schemes" (2 Corinthians 2:11). We don't want the devil to use our loss and grief to deter us in our walk with God to heaven.

Also, in prayer we might just want to pour out our hearts to the Lord. That seems to be what the author of this psalm is doing. We don't see him asking God for anything other than an attentive ear and a speedy reply. He is just telling God what is on his mind. He's telling Him of his physical and emotional condition and speaking to Him of the daily persecution he faces from those who despise him.

Looking at this psalm, we see one in trouble who devotes a portion of his prayer to praising God for his loving concern and precious promises. He expresses confidence in God's presence and protection.

To sum up this discussion of subjects for which a Christian might pray when in distress, we know that in prayer:

- We can ask for a change in our situation

- We can express a desire to be able to handle the circumstances so that they will not get the best of us spiritually.

- We can tell the Lord whatever is on our mind.

- We can offer Him praise from a heart filled with assurance of His power and love.

In essence, we can talk to God about anything and everything. Since the prayers of faithful Christians are to God as "golden bowls full of incense" (Revelation 5:8), we can "draw near with confidence to the throne of grace, so that we may receive mercy and find grace to help in time of need" (Hebrews 4:16).

The question now is: Why would we NOT take "everything to God in prayer"? Why would we continue to carry burdens on our own shoulders rather than take them to God? With the power of prayer at the disposal of every faithful Christian, there is no good reason to keep any of our heartache bottled up inside.

There is a significant point to be made here regarding prayer. Just as the Psalmist's prayer was directed to the one true God and according to His will, our prayers must be offered in this same manner. John wrote, "This is the confidence which we have before Him, that, if we ask anything according to His will, He hears us" (1 John 5:14). Our prayers must be directed to God the Father (John 16:23) through our Mediator, Jesus Christ (1 Timothy 2:5).

When we pray as God instructed in His Word, are we guaranteed to always get the result for which we ask? Of course, we know that we will not. In this Psalm, the writer recognizes the superiority of God. He writes with an understanding that God's will is greater than his. It's this faith that leads us to say as Jesus did in the Garden of Gethsemane, "not my will, but yours be done" (Luke 22:42). That, truly, is one of the great points of comfort in prayer. We admit to the Lord that we don't know what to do, that we don't understand, and that we are weak and then we take comfort in the knowledge that we are speaking to the One who knows what to do, who understands, and who is strong.

Sometimes we sing the words, "where could I go but to the Lord?" The theme of the song is that there is no other source than God for real strength, hope, and comfort. An implied lesson that is just as powerful is the fact that while those outside of Christ have nowhere to turn in their search for comfort, Christians do have the Lord to whom we can go in prayer. Indeed, where else can we go when loss and grief attack us? Turning to God should be our first thought, not an afterthought.

Key Takeaways from Chapter 13

- God is a patient listener.
- God wants to hear from us in prayer.
- God wants us to cast our cares (anxieties) on Him.

Moments of Meditation

1. Have you had moments in your grief that were so severe that you couldn't eat or sleep?

   _____

   _____

2. What happened that triggered these particular feelings?

   _____

   _____

   _____

   _____

3. What should we pray for in regard to our loss and grief?

_____

_____

_____

_____

_____

4. What does it mean if God doesn't answer our prayers the way we want and in our time frame?

_____

_____

_____

_____

_____

5. Why is it important to have the attitude of "not my will, but God's be done" in prayer?

_____

_____

_____

_____

_____

QUICK TIP

When you feel you are ready for more interaction with others following your loss, consider volunteering. There are likely many opportunities right there in your community. This can give you some insights on how others are dealing with the challenges in their lives.

Chapter Fourteen
Psalm 103
Comfort in Forgiveness

[1] Bless the LORD, O my soul, and all that is within me, *bless* His holy name.

[2] Bless the LORD, O my soul, and forget none of His benefits;

[3] Who pardons all your iniquities, who heals all your diseases;

[4] Who redeems your life from the pit, who crowns you with lovingkindness and compassion;

[5] Who satisfies your years with good things, so that your youth is renewed like the eagle.

[6] The LORD performs righteous deeds and judgments for all who are oppressed.

[7] He made known His ways to Moses, His acts to the sons of Israel.

[8] The LORD is compassionate and gracious, slow to anger and abounding in lovingkindness.

[9] He will not always strive *with us*, nor will He keep *His anger* forever.

[10] He has not dealt with us according to our sins, nor rewarded us according to our iniquities.

[11] For as high as the heavens are above the earth, so great is His lovingkindness toward those who fear Him.

[12] As far as the east is from the west, so far has He removed our transgressions from us.

[13] Just as a father has compassion on *his* children, so the LORD has compassion on those who fear Him.

[14] For He Himself knows our frame; He is mindful that we are *but* dust.

[15] As for man, his days are like grass; as a flower of the field, so he flourishes.

[16] When the wind has passed over it, it is no more, and its place acknowledges it no longer.

[17] But the lovingkindness of the LORD is from everlasting to everlasting on those who fear Him, and His righteousness to children's children,

[18] To those who keep His covenant and remember His precepts to do them.

[19] The LORD has established His throne in the heavens, and His sovereignty rules over all.

[20] Bless the LORD, you His angels, mighty in strength, who perform His word, obeying the voice of His word!

[21] Bless the LORD, all you His hosts, you who serve Him, doing His will.

[22] Bless the LORD, all you works of His, in all places of His dominion; bless the LORD, O my soul!

Examination of the Psalm

Of all the words in the English language that lift the heart and lighten the soul, few can compare to "forgiveness." It's one of the many blessings from God highlighted by the writer of this psalm.

All of the blessings listed are outstanding. Those blessings include:

- Healing (verse 3)

- Redemption (verse 4)

- Physical blessings (verse 5)

- Relief from oppression (verse 6)

Not only does the Psalmist list God's blessings, but he also notes the following characteristics of God:

- Compassionate (verse 8)

- Gracious (verse 8)

- Slow to anger (verse 8)

- Abounding in lovingkindness (verses 8 and 11)

As you read through the list of blessings and the characteristics of God, it becomes clear that everything in the psalm is pointing to the blessing of forgiveness. Without forgiveness from God, there is no salvation.

The writer's description of the completeness of God's salvation is unrivaled in beauty. Notice verse twelve. "As far as the east is from the west, so far has He removed our transgressions from us." If you were to start from where you are right now and travel north, you would go quite a distance and eventually reach the northernmost point of the globe. Upon taking your very next step, you would be heading southward. Were you to continue on this journey to the southernmost point of the globe, your very next step after you reached that point would be northward. On the other hand, were you to start from where you are right now and travel east, you would move in that direction indefinitely. Were you to begin traveling west, you would move in that direction indefinitely. East and west do not meet as north and south do. They are directions that are totally separate from one another. God's forgiveness causes the sins of one who obeys Him to be totally separated from the soul.

God's forgiveness is paramount, not only to our eternal welfare, but also to our success in overcoming life's troubles. As the writer says in verse ten, "He has not dealt with us according to our sins, nor rewarded us according to our iniquities."

In verses fourteen through sixteen, the writer reminds us of the brevity of life. Notice how he immediately follows that fact with the truth regarding the everlasting mercy of God toward them who fear and obey Him. Indeed, God is eminently worthy of the multiple exhortations the Psalmist gives to "bless" (speak well of) the Lord.

Application

The apostle Paul wrote, "There is none righteous, not even one" (Romans 3:10) and "For all have sinned and fall short of the glory of God" (Romans 3:23). Were it not for God's forgiveness, our struggles with life's difficulties would be compounded by the burden of sin. There would be nowhere to turn. Paul said in defense of the resurrection of Christ from the dead, "If we have hoped in Christ in this life only, we are of all men most to be pitied" (1 Corinthians 15:19). If there is no forgiveness with God, we also have cause to walk through life in misery. But there IS forgiveness with God and thoughts of being pure and holy in Him provide comfort that is beyond compare.

While we're on the subject of forgiveness as it relates to comfort, let's briefly consider two other points. In both of these matters, if forgiveness does not take place, sorrow will swell and comfort will not come.

The first point is in regard to the need for each of us to forgive one another. Grudge-holding is a weighty burden that can rob a person of joy and peace.

In Matthew 18:23-35 Jesus told a parable of two servants. One owed a great debt to his master. He begged for relief of the debt and his plea was granted. The other servant owed a small debt to the first servant. The first servant would not forgive that small debt. He had forgotten what his master had done for him. Jesus said,

> And his lord, moved with anger, handed him over to the torturers until he should repay all that was owed him. My heavenly Father will also do the same to you, if each of you does not forgive his brother from your heart (Matthew 18:34-35).

If we are the recipients of God's forgiveness, should we not be as generous with our forgiveness of others? "Be kind to one another, tender-hearted, forgiving each other, just as God in Christ also has forgiven you" (Ephesians 4:32).

True comfort can never come to the heart of one who is unwilling to forgive. How well I remember standing beside the hospital bed of an elderly lady who had spent years nursing a grudge against a family member. In the hours prior to her death, she repeatedly whispered, "God forgive me. God forgive me." She desperately sought the forgiveness that she herself had refused to grant for such a long time.

The second point concerns the need to forgive ourselves. One of the greatest torments we suffer in the midst of life's difficulties is that of blaming ourselves for everything that has happened. Granted, sometimes our circumstances can be the result of our actions or lack of

101

action. Even in those instances, if we seek God's forgiveness according to His will and He forgives us, we still must learn how to forgive ourselves. What I'm talking about here is the danger of constantly beating ourselves up regarding the difficulty in which we find ourselves.

Guilt becomes an aggressive enemy after a loss. We all play "what if" in our minds after a loss until it nearly overwhelms us. It doesn't end the day of or even the week after the loss either. Weeks, months, perhaps years later we might find ourselves questioning our decisions, wondering how things could have been different, tearing ourselves up emotionally regarding something over which, in reality, we had little or no control. We can't change the past. Why torment our hearts with constant repetition of scenarios that never will happen?

Seeking forgiveness, extending forgiveness, and accepting forgiveness form a magnificent trio of comfort. When one knows that he or she is forgiven, there is nothing that can keep that person in despair.

Key Takeaways from Chapter 14

- All who are accountable to God have sinned and fallen short of His glory.
- God's forgiveness is complete.
- We must learn to forgive others and forgive ourselves.

Moments of Meditation

1. If there was someone who had a part in creating the loss that you're grieving, why is it important for you to forgive that person?

_____

_____

_____

_____

_____

2. Why is it important for God to forgive you?

_____

_____

_____

_____

_____

3. Even if your loss wasn't your fault, what could you have done to prevent it?

_____

_____

_____

_____

_____

4. Whether or not you could have done anything to prevent your loss, are you beating yourself up over it?

_____

_____

_____

_____

5. If you answered "yes" to the previous question, what can you do to forgive yourself?

_____

_____

_____

_____

_____

It's okay to say "no." Well-meaning friends may try to help handle your grief by inviting you to social gatherings. You, on the other hand, might not be ready emotionally. Of course, you don't want to spend the rest of your life locked up in your house, but if you don't think you would feel comfortable at an event, don't hesitate to decline the invitation. Decline politely, perhaps even asking your friend to check back with you prior to the date of the next event.

Chapter Fifteen
Psalm 116
Comfort in Persistence

[1] I love the LORD, because He hears my voice *and* my supplications.

[2] Because He has inclined His ear to me, therefore I shall call *upon Him* as long as I live.

[3] The cords of death encompassed me and the terrors of Sheol came upon me; I found distress and sorrow.

[4] Then I called upon the name of the LORD: "O LORD, I beseech You, save my life!"

[5] Gracious is the Lord, and righteous; yes, our God is compassionate.

[6] The Lord preserves the simple; I was brought low, and He saved me.

[7] Return to your rest, O my soul, for the LORD has dealt bountifully with you.

[8] For You have rescued my soul from death, my eyes from tears, my feet from stumbling.

[9] I shall walk before the LORD in the land of the living.

[10] I believed when I said, "I am greatly afflicted."

[11] I said in my alarm, "All men are liars."

[12] What shall I render to the LORD for all His benefits toward me?

[13] I shall lift up the cup of salvation and call upon the name of the LORD.

[14] I shall pay my vows to the LORD, oh *may it be* in the presence of all His people.

[15] Precious in the sight of the LORD is the death of His godly ones.

[16] O LORD, surely I am Your servant, I am Your servant, the son of Your handmaid, You have loosed my bonds.

[17] To You I shall offer a sacrifice of thanksgiving, and call upon the name of the LORD.

¹⁸ I shall pay my vows to the LORD, oh *may it be* in the presence of all His people,
¹⁹ In the courts of the LORD's house, in the midst of you, O Jerusalem. Praise the LORD!

Examination of the Psalm

The first two verses of this Psalm speak of the writer's determination to follow God. The Lord heard him when he cried out for help.

The depth of his sorrow is seen in the words he used to describe it in verse 3. He was surrounded by "the cords of death." "The terrors of Sheol" afflicted him. He found "distress and sorrow." (verse 3). In spite of these severe challenges, he would not quit on the One who had rescued his soul from death, tears, and stumbling.

In verse 9, the writer again expresses his determination to walk with God. "I shall walk before the Lord in the land of the living." In his sorrows, pains, trouble and afflictions, he found God. As was noted in another chapter, God was there for him at all times. He just needed to recognize the fact that he could go to the Lord at all times. When the Psalmist saw how great God had been to him in all of his difficulties, he stated his intention to be persistent in relying on the One who could deliver him in his struggles.

It's interesting, but certainly not coincidental, that this psalm contains the passage often heard at funerals. "Precious in the sight of the Lord is the death of his godly ones" (verse 15). In the context of a psalm that shows the writer's commitment to God and God's commitment to him, this verse speaks of the ultimate comfort that is found in turning to God. While on earth, the Psalmist realized God's comfort in a variety of situations. This life of daily faithfulness to God finds its reward in death. Rather than defeat, saints of God find victory in passing from this life to the next.

Application

Again, this is noted in another chapter, but it doesn't hurt to be reminded that God is always there for us just as He was for the Psalmist. The question is, "Are we always looking for God?" In our struggles with loss and grief, will we try to handle them alone or will we turn to the God of all comfort? Will we persist in our faith in God even while our troubles mount and the detractors try to pull us away from the Lord?

In Luke's Gospel account, we find two powerful parables illustrating the importance of persistence. In Luke 11:1-13, we find Jesus' disciples coming to Him with a request to teach them how to pray. He proceeded to give them the essentials of acceptable prayer. Jesus then added an important component of prayer in verses five through eight when He gave an example of a person who continually asked a friend for something that he needed until he received it. The important component was and still is persistence.

The other parable in Luke's account is in Luke 18:1-8. There Jesus tells of a woman who went over and over to a judge whom she trusted could handle a matter for her that she needed resolved. In the parable, the judge granted her request. Verse eight asks a thought-provoking question. "However, when the Son of man comes, will He find faith on the earth?" In other words, will the Lord see this type of persistence in people's spiritual lives? Will those who claim to follow God through Christ be determined enough to go to Him at all times and in all situations? The comfort is there, as is the peace, the joy, the hope, the strength. Will we persist in our pursuit of God's will and His blessings?

Life's challenges afford us numerous opportunities to show our faith in God, not only to others and to God Himself, but to ourselves as well. Have you ever wondered what you would do in a certain situation? Maybe you've been at the side of someone who is struggling and either said or thought to yourself, "I don't know what I'd do if I were in your shoes." Not that we're looking for troubles, but when they do come (and they will), we are able to see for ourselves what we will do. We are also able to see for ourselves just how faithful the Lord can be to us if we will be faithful to Him. It's that persistence in the good times that aids us in being persistent in tough times.

But when this perishable will have put on the imperishable, and this mortal will have put on immortality, then will come about the saying that is written, Death is swallowed up in victory. O death, where is your victory? O death, where is your sting? The sting of death is sin, and the power of sin is the law; but thanks be to God, who gives us the victory through our Lord Jesus Christ. (1 Corinthians 15:54-57).

Key Takeaways from Chapter 15

- Being persistent in faithfulness to God will result in eternal life in heaven.
- Persistence means being faithful to God no matter how difficult life may get.
- God is faithful to His promises.

Moments of Meditation

1. What can you learn about yourself, your friends, and even God from your loss and grief?

_____

_____

_____

_____

_____

2. Where is God when you are feeling the pain of your loss?

_____

_____

_____

3. How have you responded to any temptations to quit serving God because of your loss and grief?

_____

_____

_____

_____

_____

4. Who or what should we allow to stand between us and God?

_____

_____

_____

_____

_____

5. How do we demonstrate persistence?

_____

_____

_____

_____

Be prepared for the "firsts." The "firsts" include things like your first Christmas without your spouse, your first time coming home without your pet there to greet you, etc. Try to anticipate each "first" so that you'll be emotionally ready to handle them when they occur.

Chapter Sixteen
Psalm 118
The Comfort of Knowing that I Will Win

¹ Give thanks to the LORD, for He is good; for His lovingkindness is everlasting.

² Oh let Israel say, "His lovingkindness is everlasting."

³ Oh let the house of Aaron say, "His lovingkindness is everlasting."

⁴ Oh let those who fear the LORD say, "His lovingkindness is everlasting."

⁵ From my distress I called upon the LORD; The LORD answered me *and set me* in a large place.

⁶ The LORD is for me; I will not fear; what can man do to me?

⁷ The LORD is for me among those who help me; therefore I will look *with satisfaction* on those who hate me.

⁸ It is better to take refuge in the LORD than to trust in man.

⁹ It is better to take refuge in the LORD than to trust in princes.

¹⁰ All nations surrounded me; in the name of the LORD I will surely cut them off.

¹¹ They surrounded me, yes, they surrounded me; in the name of the LORD I will surely cut them off.

¹² They surrounded me like bees; they were extinguished as a fire of thorns; in the name of the LORD I will surely cut them off.

¹³ You pushed me violently so that I was falling, but the LORD helped me.

¹⁴ The LORD is my strength and song, and He has become my salvation.

¹⁵ The sound of joyful shouting and salvation is in the tents of the righteous; the right hand of the LORD does valiantly.

¹⁶ The right hand of the LORD is exalted; the right hand of the LORD does valiantly.

¹⁷ I will not die, but live, and tell of the works of the LORD.

¹⁸ The LORD has disciplined me severely, but He has not given me over to death.

^{19} Open to me the gates of righteousness; I shall enter through them, I shall give thanks to the LORD.

^{20} This is the gate of the LORD; the righteous will enter through it.

^{21} I shall give thanks to You, for You have answered me, and You have become my salvation.

^{22} The stone which the builders rejected has become the chief corner *stone*.

^{23} This is the LORD's doing; it is marvelous in our eyes.

^{24} This is the day which the LORD has made; let us rejoice and be glad in it.

^{25} O LORD, do save, we beseech You; O LORD, we beseech You, do send prosperity!

^{26} Blessed is the one who comes in the name of the LORD; we have blessed you from the house of the LORD.

^{27} The LORD is God, and He has given us light; bind the festival sacrifice with cords to the horns of the altar.

^{28} You are my God, and I give thanks to You; *You are* my God, I extol You.

^{29} Give thanks to the LORD, for He is good; for His lovingkindness is everlasting.

Examination of the Psalm

Despite the length of this psalm, it really doesn't require much commentary regarding the comfort it provides for the hurting heart. Very simply, it is a psalm of victory. A brief phrase in verse five ("From my distress I called upon the Lord") and a few sentences in verses 10 through 13 show that the Psalmist had been suffering. In verse 18, the writer speaks of how the Lord had disciplined him. Other than that, there is nothing but excitement in the writer's heart and exultation in his inspired words. He has seen the victory that God provides and He wants others to know of the merciful God who delivers the righteous from their troubles.

That victory is not found in the words of men. The power of princes cannot provide deliverance. Salvation is in Jehovah God. "The right hand of the Lord" (a term representing strength) is alone sufficient to free the faithful from whatever distresses them. The joy of salvation in the Lord is emphasized three separate times, with a prophecy of the Christ who would come and be the culmination of God's plan for salvation found in verse 22. The Psalmist urges adoration of the Father. He is the one true God. He alone is worthy of praise. He is the source of victory over the challenges of life, no matter what they may be or how or from whom they may come.

Application

Doubtless, there have been times when each of us wished we could have known the outcome of a situation in advance. If only we could have seen how things would turn out, we would have felt much better and more capable of handling the challenge as we wrestled with it.

The fact is that we do know the outcome. We may not know the particulars, but we do "know that God causes all things to work together for good to those who love God, to those who are called according to His purpose" (Romans 8:28). We know that our challenges will make us stronger if we let them (2 Corinthians 12:7-11; Philippians 4:11-13). We know that the Lord will be at our side through the battle and we are confident that He will be there at the end of it (Hebrews 13:5). We can say with the inspired writer, "The Lord is on my side; I will not fear."

This psalm is a microcosm of life as a whole. Life's distresses come at us, sometimes with the ferocity of the bees to which the writer refers in verse 12. The Lord has given His Word and has His ears open to the prayers of the faithful (Revelation 5:8). He will deliver again and again, lifting up the fallen, binding the wounds of those who hurt, and cheering the hearts of the fainting. Each challenge will be overcome by those who walk faithfully with God and ultimately, life's biggest challenge, that of sin and its destructiveness, will be overcome in eternity (Revelation 14:13).

The Psalm is also a microcosm of the Bible as a whole. Victory stands out as the focal point of God's Word. Genesis 1:31 speaks of God's perfect creation. Soon marred by sin (Genesis 3:6), this creation appeared to be forever severed from fellowship with the Lord (Isaiah

59:1-2). But hope for victory is announced early on in Genesis 3:15. Throughout the pages of the Bible, this hope is fostered through the words of inspired men. The Word contains numerous accounts of individuals rising, then falling, and then rising again to be close to God. Finally, just before the pen of Divine inspiration was laid down once and for all, the apostle John wrote of ultimate victory in eternity in Revelation 22. Follow God's Word from beginning to end and you will see the path of victory for those who follow the Lord.

If God can provide eternal victory over sin, He can provide victory over the challenges we face in life. Must we allow loss and grief to defeat us? Not at all. Indeed, the struggles are real and the pain is intense. At times, it seems that we will never get over it. But the faithful will win. The difficulties of life are short-lived. After enumerating some of the trials he had undergone, Paul wrote:

> Therefore we do not lose heart, but though our outer man is decaying, yet our inner man is being renewed day by day. For momentary, light affliction is producing for us an eternal weight of glory far beyond all comparison, while we look not at the things which are seen, but at the things which are not seen; for the things which are seen are temporal, but the things which are not seen are eternal. For we know that if the earthly tent which is our house is torn down, we have a building from God, a house not made with hands, eternal in the heavens. (2 Corinthians 4:16-5:1).

Even if trials continue throughout life, there is ultimately a release and eternal relief for the faithful Christian.

The faithful will win. Why? Going back to the Psalm under consideration in this chapter, we find the following reasons:

- "He (God) is good."

- "His (God's) lovingkindness is everlasting."

- "The Lord is my strength and song, and He has become my salvation."

114

- "The right hand of the Lord is exalted; the right hand of the Lord does valiantly."

- "The Lord is on my side; I will not fear."

There is no distress so great, no sorrow so deep, no anguish so severe that Satan will not try to use it to turn us away from following God. He tried to turn Job's difficulties into a victory for evil. Many times, he sought victory over Joseph (Genesis 37ff). He even tried his hand at defeating Jesus (Matthew 4:1-11).

Much to Satan's chagrin, there is no distress so great, no sorrow so deep, no anguish so severe that God cannot provide the victory over it in the heart of the faithful Christian. The faithful will win. The sadness may linger, and the heart may feel the pangs of grief for many a day or year, but the faithful will overcome.

Jesus said, "These things I have spoken to you, so that in Me you may have peace. In the world you have tribulation, but take courage; I have overcome the world" (John 16:33). John himself would later write about overcoming. "I am writing to you, young men, because you have overcome the evil one…" (1 John 2:13). "… and the word of God abides in you, and you have overcome the evil one" (1 John 2:14). "Ye are from God, little children, and have overcome them; because greater is He who is in you than He who is in the world" (1 John 4:4).

As downtrodden and broken in heart as we might feel due to loss and grief, if we are faithful Christians, we will win. "For whatever is born of God overcomes the world; and this is the victory that has overcome the world - our faith" (1 John 5:4). "Give thanks to the Lord, for He is good; for His lovingkindness is everlasting."

Key Takeaways from Chapter 16

- God is the source of victory over the challenges of life.
- Those who are faithful to God will have the ultimate victory in heaven.
- There is great joy in serving God.

Moments of Meditation

1. How can a positive attitude help us recover from loss and grief?

    _____

    _____

    _____

    _____

    _____

2. How do thoughts of victory in heaven help develop a positive attitude?

    _____

    _____

    _____

    _____

    _____

3. What can we do to grow and maintain a positive attitude?

    _____

4. List three examples of how God has been good to you.

5. What are you thankful for today?

Dealing with grief after a loss can often feel like riding a roller coaster. You're up one day and down the next. Be mindful of the uncertainty that comes with grief. Don't let the "down" days discourage you. There will be "up" days to follow.

Chapter Seventeen
Psalm 120
Comfort Even in the Presence
of Negative Influences

[1] In my trouble I cried to the LORD, and He answered me.
[2] Deliver my soul, O LORD, from lying lips, from a deceitful tongue.
[3] What shall be given to you, and what more shall be done to you, you deceitful tongue?
[4] Sharp arrows of the warrior, with the *burning* coals of the broom tree.
[5] Woe is me, for I sojourn in Meshech, for I dwell among the tents of Kedar!
[6] Too long has my soul had its dwelling with those who hate peace.
[7] I am *for* peace, but when I speak, they are for war.

Examination of the Psalm

In this Psalm, the writer gives us a glimpse into the society in which he lived. He was surrounded by liars and deceivers whose false tongues inflicted pain and suffering upon the hearts of those subjected to their evil ways. It was a sorrowful situation in which he found himself. He wanted to live a peaceful, God-fearing life but he was constantly at odds with those around him who desired an entirely different lifestyle. Despite his many detractors, the Psalmist still found God and relied on Him for deliverance from his woes.

Application

As strange as it may seem, there are those who will use another person's suffering as an opportunity to inflict even more pain. The phrase, "kicking a person while he's down" didn't appear out of thin air.

Undoubtedly, someone who had felt the "kick" came up with that phrase.

The most obvious example of this "kicking" is found in the book of Job. After losing his possessions, his children, and even his health, Job was greeted by three men who are called his friends in Job 2:11. At first it seems that they were sympathetic toward him in his loss. Job 2:12 states, "When they lifted up their eyes at a distance and did not recognize him, they raised their voices and wept. And each of them tore his robe and they threw dust over their heads toward the sky." Job 2:13 says that they sat in silence with Job for seven days and nights "for they saw that his pain was very great."

When Job finally opened his mouth, he spoke of his great sadness, even wishing that he had never been born (Job 3). Rather than allowing Job to vent his anguish and frustration over his losses, Eliphaz, one of the three, basically told Job, "I just have to say something." (Job 4:2). He spoke of how Job had helped others in their trouble and added, "But now it has come to you, and you are impatient; it touches you, and you are dismayed" (Job 4:5).

Then Eliphaz delivered the key blow that emanated from the thoughts he had kept to himself for at least those seven days of silence. "Remember now, who ever perished being innocent? Or where were the upright destroyed? According to what I have seen, those who plow iniquity and those who sow trouble harvest it" (Job 4:7-8). In other words, "Job, you are obviously getting what you deserve. No one suffers unless they have done something terribly wrong." As book of Job progresses, we find Eliphaz, along with the other two friends, Bildad and Zophar, continuing this line of reasoning while Job defends his faithfulness to God.

Even though Job showed some weakness and was reprimanded by God for his attitude (Job 38-42), he nonetheless continued returning to the Lord in search of answers. He refused to renounce his faith, even when his wife encouraged him to do so (Job 2:9-10). Indeed, the Lord had well said of Job, "there is no one like him on the earth, a blameless and upright man, fearing God and turning away from evil" (Job 1:8).

Loss and grief can take many forms. Physical illness or the death of a loved one, our own physical illness, financial straits, discord in the home, and issues on the job are just a few of the situations in which we can experience troubles. In each of these we do well in seeking comfort from the Lord, but in each of these there lies the possibility of encountering those who would discourage us from relying on God.

Here's a person who has lost a loved one to sudden death. As this individual struggles to come to grips with the loss, he or she is confronted by friends and family who are angry and who are not taking their grief to God. They may say, "I can't believe you are taking this so calmly. How could you trust a God who would allow this to happen?"

Here's a person who has lost just about everything due to no fault of his or her own. As he or she commits this sorrow and anguish to God, friends and family begin to blame the person for poor business decisions. Others crank up the gossip machine and run it at full speed.

Here's someone whose family is in shambles. While that individual seeks God amidst the heartache of a broken home, friends and family point fingers. "This never would have happened had you…." "I know what I would have done if my family had gotten like that..."

Thankfully, there are countless numbers of friends and family who will stand with us and share in our requests to God for comfort. Nonetheless, we may encounter, as Job did, those who are "worthless physicians" (Job 13:4). Not only will they try to discourage us, but they will also try to shift our focus and turn our eyes away from God.

The inspired writer of this psalm found God even though those around him showed no concern for the Lord. He cried out to the Lord in his distress and was heard.

Job found God, even though his wife urged him to "curse God, and die" (Job 2:9) and his companions essentially told him that God wanted nothing to do with so vile a sinner. Job 42:12 opens with, "The Lord blessed the latter days of Job more than his beginning."

When we face loss and grief, we can find the God of all comfort just as easily as we can find Him in good times, regardless of what those around us may say or do. As Jesus said, "Ask, and it will be given to you; seek, and you will find; knock, and it will be opened to you. For everyone who asks receives, and he who seeks finds, and to him who knocks it will be opened" (Matthew 7:7-8).

"Let all who seek You rejoice and be glad in You; let those who love Your salvation say continually, 'The Lord be magnified!'" (Psalm 40:16).

Key Takeaways from Chapter 17

- Sometimes people will try to drag us down and make our grief even worse.
- On the other hand, there are always friends and family who will encourage us and be there for us.
- God is always nearby.

Moments of Meditation

1. How can we keep negative people from influencing us?

   _____

   _____

   _____

   _____

   _____

2. How could you politely ask someone to not be so negative in their comments to you?

   _____

_____

_____

_____

_____

3. In what ways are negative thoughts potentially harmful to us as we recover from a loss?

_____

_____

_____

_____

_____

4. What is the meaning of Romans 8:31? ("What then shall we say to these things? If God is for us, who is against us?")

_____

_____

_____

_____

_____

5. How can the way we handle our loss have a positive impact on others?

_____

_____

_____

_____

_____

Set goals for your recovery and write them down. The purpose of this is to keep you moving forward. Be specific. Describe each goal. What is the purpose of it? Specify the date when you will achieve it. Write down the details of what you want to accomplish through this goal. Envision how you will feel after you reach each goal. Be aware of your limitations. You're not going to recover from loss and grief overnight. Setting a series of small goals that lead to a larger goal can work well and can keep you from feeling overwhelmed.

Chapter Eighteen
Psalm 121
Comfort in God's Preservation

[1] I will lift up my eyes to the mountains; from where shall my help come?

[2] My help *comes* from the LORD, Who made heaven and earth.

[3] He will not allow your foot to slip; He who keeps you will not slumber.

[4] Behold, He who keeps Israel will neither slumber nor sleep.

[5] The LORD is your keeper; the LORD is your shade on your right hand.

[6] The sun will not smite you by day, nor the moon by night.

[7] The LORD will protect you from all evil; He will keep your soul.

[8] The LORD will guard your going out and your coming in from this time forth and forever.

Examination of the Psalm

This is another brief psalm that requires little explanation. Its message is clear. God watches over and takes care of His people. What's most impressive about this Psalm is the number of times a single Hebrew word is used in just a few short verses. Six different times this particular word is used, three times being translated "keeps" or "keep," once "keeper," once "protect," and once "guard." In the opening verses, the writer acknowledges the source of any help he has received. The Lord above is the source. The God who made heaven and earth is the origin of true and sufficient help. This God shows His dedication to His followers by never turning away from them. He never rests but is ever watchful over His people. He is the keeper, the source of preservation for those who abide in Him.

Application

The Hebrew word noted in the previous paragraph is found over 460 times in the Old Testament. It carries with it a broad array of definitions, but they all come down to the idea of guarding, observing, giving heed, watching, preserving, and protecting. In essence, God is watching over His faithful followers.

In the chapter on Psalm 23 we considered the fact that God knows us. Perhaps there are some similarities between these two chapters in this book, but the emphasis here is more on the fact that God sees all in our lives. Psalm 23 implies that He sees all because it shows how the Lord provides all that we need. This Psalm devotes more of itself to plainly stating that God sees all.

Does God know when we hurt? Is He watching when bad things happen to His people? Is He aware of the struggles that we face in trying to adjust to the dramatic changes in our lives brought on by loss and grief? The repetition of the word that shows God is watching, observing, and giving heed to our lives indicates that He is indeed aware of every moment, both good and bad, in our lives. Such a thought was warmly welcomed by this Psalmist. He knew where to find God. He knew that God saw him in the daytime and in the evening and whether he was going or coming. He took comfort in the knowledge that the ever-seeing eye of the Lord was aware of his every step. He took comfort in this because he knew that along with this watchfulness came the strength to stand firm and the preservation against evil. Nothing could really harm him as long as his God was watching over him. When he needed help, he knew where to find its source.

Knowing that God is ever present is disturbing to those who don't want Him to see what they're doing. To those who want to serve Him faithfully, such knowledge is worth more than any treasure on earth. While it is true that there is no sinful thought or evil deed that God does not see, it's also true that there is no act of righteousness of which He is not aware and there is no twinge of sadness that is not laid bare before Him.

Psalm 139 adds to the beauty of this thought about God's omnipresence and omniscience. There the Psalmist wrote,

> Where can I go from Your Spirit? Or where can I flee from Your presence? If I ascend to heaven, You are there; If I make my bed in Sheol, behold, You are there. If I take the wings of the dawn, if I dwell in the remotest part of the sea, even there Your hand will lead me, and Your right hand will lay hold of me. If I say, "Surely the darkness will overwhelm me, and the light around me will be night," Even the darkness is not dark to You, and the night is as bright as the day. Darkness and light are alike to You. (Psalm 139:7-12)

God sees when we hurt. Some might wonder that since this is the case, why doesn't God do something to prevent the pain. After all, is the Psalmist not saying here that God will keep His people from all things harmful? That's a good question. Is he suggesting that God suspends all laws of nature in order to keep anything bad from happening to His people? Is he indicating that God puts a halt to the aging process so that no one will ever get sick, grow old and die?

What the Psalmist seems to be saying is that while God watches over us physically, He also preserves, guards, and protects us spiritually. The former is obvious because the Psalmist is writing to living people. The latter is determined by the context, especially verse seven in which he has written, "he will keep your soul." God is watching over us and He will preserve, guard, and give heed to the spiritual welfare of those who rely on Him. Philippians 4:6-7 attests to this.

> Be anxious for nothing, but in everything by prayer and supplication with thanksgiving let your requests be made known to God. And the peace of God, which surpasses all comprehension, will guard your hearts and your minds in Christ Jesus.

As much as the difficulties of life hurt, they don't have to destroy us. The challenges will come, and God sees when they do come, but He has established His guard to preserve us during these times. The troubles may become intense, but they will not smite our souls if we keep a firm foothold in God's Word. No matter where we may go, or how long we may live, we will have God's preservation of our souls if we faithfully obey His Word.

God's constant watchfulness and loving preservation are two facts that support the inherent power that lies in acceptable prayer. Hebrews 4:13 reads, "And there is no creature hidden from His sight, but all things are open and laid bare to the eyes of Him with whom we have to do." Since God is always watching us, then He is always near in prayer. Paul said, "that they would seek God, if perhaps they might grope for Him and find Him, though He is not far from each one of us" (Acts 17:27). The Lord is not far off. Paul wrote in Philippians 4:5 that He is at hand. We may not be able to see Him, but He can see us.

Who among us can tell when and where the pains of sadness will strike during our time of grief following a loss? We could go for days feeling happy and content and then suddenly, a song, a scent, a picture, practically anything could usher in a wave of sorrow and a rush of tears. As is clearly indicated in Psalm 121, God is there, and He sees that. Since He is there, He is available in prayer. We can express the depths of our sorrow to Him in prayer and supplication, assured that He is dedicated to the preservation of our souls.

Key Takeaways from Chapter 18

- God watches over and takes care of His people.
- God knows when we are hurting.
- As much as the difficulties of life hurt, they don't have to destroy us.

Moments of Meditation

1. How does God guard us?

_____

_____

_____

_____

2. How does it help to know that God is aware of our pain?

_____

_____

_____

_____

3. Why is God concerned about our spiritual welfare?

_____

_____

_____

_____

4. What did Paul mean when he said that God "is not far from each one of us" in Acts 17:27?

_____

_____

_____

_____

_____

5. What is the meaning of, "Draw near to God and He will draw near to you?" (James 4:8).

_____

_____

_____

_____

_____

Be aware of reminders of your loss. If you find yourself suddenly sad for no apparent reason, stop and think about why you feel that way. Once you isolate its cause, see if you can turn that trigger for sadness into a trigger for happiness. For example, you might cry if you smell a cologne that your deceased loved one wore. Make a written note of this incident and then write down some positive memories associated with it. The next time it happens, you are likely to begin thinking about happy memories rather than sad ones.

Chapter Nineteen
Psalm 130
Comfort in Waiting for the Lord

¹ Out of the depths I have cried to You, O LORD.

² Lord, hear my voice! Let Your ears be attentive to the voice of my supplications.

³ If You, Lord, should mark iniquities, O LORD, who could stand?

⁴ But there is forgiveness with You, that You may be feared.

⁵ I wait for the LORD, my soul does wait, and in His word do I hope.

⁶ My soul *waits* for the Lord more than the watchmen for the morning; *indeed, more than* the watchmen for the morning.

⁷ O Israel, hope in the LORD; for with the LORD there is lovingkindness, and with Him is abundant redemption.

⁸ And He will redeem Israel from all his iniquities.

Examination of the Psalm

This Psalm begins with the writer in those familiar depths which have been mentioned in other Psalms and which we ourselves have experienced. How many times have we felt that our hearts had reached the lowest regions of despair? The positive side of finding ourselves in such a state is that, if we have hit the bottom, there's nowhere to go but up! This is the Psalmist's attitude. From his depths he doesn't look down to see how much further he might fall. Instead, he looks above to the Lord whom he trusts to deliver him from his miry pit of sorrow. He pleads for the Lord's attention. He counts on the Lord in His mercy to open His ears and answer his prayer. With that in mind, he expresses the patience that is the theme of the Psalm and the focus of this chapter. Because he is calling upon the merciful God, the Psalmist is willing to be patient for an answer. He will be like one who through the night anxiously looks forward to the sunrise, but he will be patient because of his trust in the Lord.

Application

It may seem rather curious for a book devoted to comfort to contain a chapter about patience. What could one possibly have to do with the other? The answer is simple. Have you ever been impatient? If so, then you know the DIScomfort of stress. Impatience feeds anxiety while patience fosters trust which, in turn, brings comfort. Nothing tests our patience more than life's challenges.

We don't want to hurt. We want relief and we want it now. The trouble is that too often we expect life to be like a television show. A typical thirty- or sixty-minute program begins with a problem, proceeds to show that problem being addressed, and then closes with it being solved, all within that time frame. Life should be so easy. The fact is, however, that relief from the difficulties we are facing frequently takes time to develop, thus demanding patience with God, with others, and with ourselves.

Other chapters in this book have referenced the goodness of God in caring for His people. We only make note of it here so as to show it as the foundation of the patience that leads to comfort. Without the loving and merciful God there would be no reason for patience because we could not expect anything good to happen to us. A cruel, vicious God would offer no hope or promise of relief from life's difficulties and would leave us nothing good to anticipate. The God of creation, however, cares for His faithful ones. As a result, we know that He will give what is best and we patiently walk with Him with this confidence.

It's strange to hear people talk about "getting over" a loss that they've faced. Do we ever really "get over" it or does the intensity of it just lessen as time moves us away from it? In the newness of the loss, we are consumed by its pain and its almost surreal nature. In the days that follow we have flashbacks of scenes of the loss and the people involved. We go through many moments of questioning why it happened and wondering if we could have done something to stop it. If the loss is the death of a loved one, we may even wonder why it wasn't us who died.

Ensuing weeks run us through a wide range of emotions from anger to guilt to loneliness (especially in the loss of a loved one). It may be only days after the event that we begin to wonder if we'll ever feel happy again or if we'll ever be able to get that loss out of our minds. Certainly, as the weeks pass and we still find ourselves thinking about what happened, our desire to move on and not keep replaying the past in our minds grows stronger. Will we ever "get over" it? When the patriarch Jacob thought his beloved son, Joseph, had been killed, he said, "Surely I will go down to Sheol in mourning for my son" (Genesis 37:35). He did not see himself ever being able to overcome his grief.

The pain can lessen, especially as we turn to God for the comfort that He provides. All of the Psalms that are the subject of the study of this book, along with countless other inspired scriptures, serve to bring us to that "peace of God, which surpasses all comprehension" (Philippians 4:7). But does the pain go away the moment we start reading God's Word? Do the tears of sorrow dry up immediately upon going to God in prayer? Because we still hurt days, weeks, months or even years after a death or some other loss in our lives, does that mean that we are weak in faith? Does it mean that God's Word is not as comforting as it is made out to be?

Think about this: Every one of the psalms being considered in this book is couched in the individual writer's need for comfort. Each writer is hurting in some way. Many of these psalms were written by one man, King David. His pain sometimes lingered. God's deliverance was sometimes not immediate. Does that mean that David did not have faith or that God was not being good to him? No, what it means is that sometimes the relief that God provides takes time. In some of the Psalms, the writers wanted relief from the oppression of the enemy. In God's master plan, this would take time. In our lives, there may be greater good that can arise from our suffering (see Job). Comfort comes and will continue to come, but the lessening of the pain may take time.

Have you ever broken a bone? If you have and you are like most people, you were in pain. How long did it take for the pain to go away? Was it immediate? Even after the medicine and the extra attention you got, you still knew you had a broken bone because that cast was a constant reminder. Even as that cast was working to mend your bone, did you not from time to time feel the discomfort of that cumbersome annoyance? As much as you wanted the bone to mend immediately, you knew it would take time.

The same is true of a broken heart. It can take time to mend. How long does it take? The answers to that question are as many in number as the people of whom it is asked. One of my Gospel preacher friends who had lost his wife to cancer told me, "Don't let anyone tell you how to grieve." That was sage advice. While we, in our grief, are trying to practice patience in our recovery, we must not allow others to rush us through the process. We need time. We need to work through the challenges we face.

In waiting for the Lord, we are not sitting around expecting Him to miraculously stir us out of our sadness. Throughout the psalm, action is combined with waiting. While waiting, the Psalmist is praying and consulting God's Word, the source of his hope (verse 5).

James gives an interesting instruction regarding patience. "And let endurance have its perfect result, so that you may be perfect and complete, lacking in nothing" (James 1:4). Let patience work. Let it develop. Why? The reason is because the more we patiently seek God, the stronger we become spiritually and emotionally.

This is a wonderful combination. Sitting around and doing nothing, looking inward at our sorrow rather than upward for our relief, will certainly lead to depression. On the other hand, the more we turn to God, the more patience we develop and the more faith we build. Job said, "But he knows the way I take; when he has tried me, I shall come forth as gold" (Job 23:10). Peter wrote, "so that the proof of your faith, being more precious than gold which is perishable, even though tested by fire, may be found to result in praise and glory and honor at the revelation of Jesus Christ" (1 Peter 1:7). Let patience work. Allow your faith and trust in God to grow through the patience that you are developing and allow your patience to develop through your faith and trust in God.

While waiting for the Lord means that we trust Him to care for us in our sorrow, it also means that we don't try to get ahead of Him. Some, in their grief, turn away from God, blaming Him for what happened. Some become despondent and give up. Some turn to drugs. Some even take their own lives. God's "divine power has granted to us everything pertaining to life and godliness, through the true knowledge of Him who called us by His own glory and excellence" (2 Peter 1:3). We have all that we need from Him. The Word that God has given us will work to comfort us if we will continually go to it and patiently apply it.

There are two other verses in the Psalms that echo the sentiment of Psalm 130. The first is Psalm 27:14. "Wait for the Lord; be strong and let your heart take courage; yes, wait for the Lord." Have you, as a parent, ever told your child to do something and then repeated it for emphasis? It's obvious that in this instruction to your child you were expressing how important it was for him to do what you said. That's the motivation behind Psalm 27:14. "Be patient. Don't get ahead of God. Be strong in Him. He will be there for you. Be patient, I said." That's a great verse. Now read it again and compare it to the Psalmist's words in Psalm 130, especially verses five and six. In Psalm 27 we find an exhortation to wait. In Psalm 130:5-6, we find a commitment to wait. Not just once or twice but three times this Psalmist says he will wait. As he waits, he hopes, knowing full well the goodness of God.

The other verse that expresses the thought of Psalm 130 is Psalm 46:10. "Cease striving and know that I am God; I will be exalted among the nations, I will be exalted in the earth." The scene that immediately comes to my mind when I read this verse is that of Moses and the Israelites as they stood on the banks of the Red Sea with the Egyptian army in hot pursuit. Afraid that they were trapped and were about to be destroyed by the Egyptians, the masses cried out. "But Moses said to the people, Do not fear! Stand by and see the salvation of the Lord which He will accomplish for you today; for the Egyptians whom you have seen today, you will never see them again forever. The Lord will fight for you while you keep silent." (Exodus 14:13-14). Being still in both settings means stop being stressed. Calm down. Be patient. Trust God. As this applies to those who are grieving, the message is regarding the need to not fret. Even though your world seems to be crumbling, God is still there. His Word is still powerful. He will still hear the prayers of the faithful. In His providence He is still active in this world. Be patient. You will find the comfort you crave.

The effort that we put forth to develop patience in the face of life's challenges is well worth the results. As is true in so many other psalms, this one speaks of a reward for patience that is far above what any trust in earthly things could produce. To the original readers, the promise was that of not just redemption, but abundant redemption. Isn't it great to know that we today can enjoy this same abundance?

Key Takeaways from Chapter 19

- Impatience feeds anxiety while patience fosters trust which, in turn, brings comfort.
- Recovering from a loss often takes time.
- The Word that God has given us will work to comfort us if we will continually go to it and patiently apply it.

Moments of Meditation

1. How does being patient lead to our comfort?

_____

_____

_____

_____

_____

2. How does being impatient lead to our discomfort?

_____

_____

_____

_____

_____

3. Do you believe that God knows what is best for you? Why or why not?

_____

_____

_____

_____

_____

4. If we believe that God knows what is best for us, what should be our attitude when we don't get what we want from Him when we want it?

_____

_____

_____

_____

_____

5. How can learning to be patient with God help us recover from loss and grief?

_____

_____

_____

_____

_____

Keep an eye on your anger and don't let it control you. As you grieve your loss, you might be tempted to start placing blame. You might blame God, friends, family members, or even yourself. Along with this desire to start pointing fingers comes anger. Prolonged anger is not productive, will slow down your recovery, and will give you a sour disposition as well as a dark outlook on life.

Chapter Twenty
Psalm 139
Comfort "24/7/365"

[1] O LORD, You have searched me and known *me*.

[2] You know when I sit down and when I rise up; You understand my thought from afar.

[3] You scrutinize my path and my lying down, and are intimately acquainted with all my ways.

[4] Even before there is a word on my tongue, behold, O LORD, You know it all.

[5] You have enclosed me behind and before, and laid Your hand upon me.

[6] Such knowledge is too wonderful for me; it is too high, I cannot attain to it.

[7] Where can I go from Your Spirit? Or where can I flee from Your presence?

[8] If I ascend to heaven, You are there; if I make my bed in Sheol, behold, You are there.

[9] If I take the wings of the dawn, if I dwell in the remotest part of the sea,

[10] Even there Your hand will lead me, and Your right hand will lay hold of me.

[11] If I say, 'Surely the darkness will overwhelm me, and the light around me will be night,'

[12] Even the darkness is not dark to You, and the night is as bright as the day. Darkness and light are alike *to You.*

[13] For You formed my inward parts; You wove me in my mother's womb.

[14] I will give thanks to You, for I am fearfully and wonderfully made; wonderful are Your works, and my soul knows it very well.

[15] My frame was not hidden from You, when I was made in secret, and skillfully wrought in the depths of the earth;

¹⁶ Your eyes have seen my unformed substance; and in Your book were all written the days that were ordained *for me*, when as yet there was not one of them.

¹⁷ How precious also are Your thoughts to me, O God! How vast is the sum of them!

¹⁸ If I should count them, they would outnumber the sand. When I awake, I am still with You.

¹⁹ O that You would slay the wicked, O God; depart from me, therefore, men of bloodshed.

²⁰ For they speak against You wickedly, and Your enemies take *Your name* in vain.

²¹ Do I not hate those who hate You, O LORD? And do I not loathe those who rise up against You?

²² I hate them with the utmost hatred; they have become my enemies.

²³ Search me, O God, and know my heart; try me and know my anxious thoughts;

²⁴ And see if there be any hurtful way in me, and lead me in the everlasting way.

Examination of the Psalm

Israel was surrounded by idolatry. Whether it was the nations around them when they were free, the Babylonian society when they were in captivity, or some of their own people in both settings, they were well acquainted with the gods that man had created.

Each of these false gods was limited in its capacity. In contrast to the false gods, the writer of Psalm 139 would have his readers understand that the true God is not limited in any way. There is not a time of day in which He is not present. There is not a thought or word that can be hidden from Him. Darkness cannot cloak the actions of His creation. The highest heights and deepest depths find Him there.

When this Psalmist considered the omnipresence of God, he wrote, "Such knowledge is too wonderful for me" (verse 6). The word "wonderful" means "incomprehensible, extraordinary." When he talks about dwelling "in the uttermost parts of the sea," in verse 9, he immediately follows that consideration with, "Even there Your hand will lead me, and Your right hand will lay hold of me." In verse eighteen, after commenting on God's thoughts, the writer says, "When I awake, I am still with You." God was there when the Psalmist went to sleep, while he slept, and when he arose in the morning. He was there, as we say in our terminology, "24/7/365."

Application

Think about this great truth as it relates to comfort. There is no situation in our lives of which our God is unaware. There is no time or place in which we cannot seek God and find Him if we seek Him according to His will (1 John 5:14-15). His Word is at our fingertips. His merciful ear is open to the prayers of the faithful (Psalm 34:15). He will not sleep (Psalm 121:3). He will not go on a journey to a distant land in which He cannot hear (Acts 17:27-28). Lovingly and tenderly, He says to His faithful ones, "I will never desert you, nor will I ever forsake you" (Hebrews 13:5).

When we're struggling with loss and grief, it's amazing how quickly we can go from a high to a low. One day we can be on top of the world with everything appearing to be going our way. The next day we can feel as though we've been abandoned.

There are so many factors that contribute to these seemingly sudden changes. A physical illness could dull our senses. Something we hear, something we see, or even something we smell could bring to mind a sad thought. Anyone who has lost a loved one knows how this feels. A certain song comes on the radio and immediately you're transported back to the time when you and that loved one were listening to that song together. You want the memory to make you happy and perhaps it does for a moment, but then you begin missing your beloved. A certain smell wafts through the air and it's almost as if the one with whom you associate that smell is in the room with you. Sadness ensues when you realize that he or she is not there. There are so many things that can trigger sadness but no matter where or when they happen, we have the God of all comfort at our side.

141

How marvelous it is to consider the fact that we can find God any time of day or night. When loss and grief strike, we can turn to God and find Him. Let us not deprive ourselves of this great blessing by limiting our contact with God to a building or an assembling with the church for worship. This is not to diminish the importance of worshipping with the saints (see this book's chapter on Psalm 95). It's just that we should not think of God as being confined to a certain place. When Solomon dedicated the temple to God he said, "But will God indeed dwell on the earth? Behold, heaven and the highest heaven cannot contain You, how much less this house which I have built!" (1 Kings 8:27).

Israelite parents were taught how to bring their children up in God's way. They were told, "These words, which I am commanding you today, shall be on your heart. You shall teach them diligently to your sons and shall talk of them when you sit in your house and when you walk by the way and when you lie down and when you rise up" (Deuteronomy 6:6-7). They were to instruct their children in righteousness at home, in their travels, at night and in the morning. When we need the comfort that only God can supply, may we follow this example and also seek Him when we're at home, when we're away from home, at nighttime and in the day. In other words, let us never limit our contact with the infinite source of comfort for He is there for us "24/7/365."

Key Takeaways from Chapter 20

- There is no situation in our lives of which our God is unaware.
- God can be found any time of day or night.
- There is no time or place in which we cannot seek God and find Him if we seek Him according to His will.

Moments of Meditation

1. How often is God available to hear prayer?

2. What are some of the blessings you are enjoying from God today?

_____

_____

_____

_____

_____

3. Why does it sometimes seem that God is not nearby?

_____

_____

_____

_____

_____

4. When should we turn to God?

_____

_____

_____

_____

_____

5. Why should we turn to God?

_____

_____

_____

_____

_____

Give yourself credit. You are stronger and more resilient than you realize. You can accomplish more than you think you can. When you reach a goal, give yourself a pat on the back or reward yourself with something like a nice walk in the park.

Chapter Twenty-One
Psalm 142
Comfort in My Refuge

¹ I cry aloud with my voice to the LORD; I make supplication with my voice to the LORD.

² I pour out my complaint before Him; I declare my trouble before Him.

³ When my spirit was overwhelmed within me, You knew my path. In the way where I walk they have hidden a trap for me.

⁴ Look to the right and see; for there is no one who regards me; there is no escape for me; No one cares for my soul.

⁵ I cried out to You, O LORD; I said, "You are my refuge, my portion in the land of the living.

⁶ "Give heed to my cry, For I am brought very low; deliver me from my persecutors, for they are too strong for me.

⁷ "Bring my soul out of prison, O that I may give thanks to Your name; The righteous will surround me, for You will deal bountifully with me."

Examination of the Psalm

Although the titles that preface many of the psalms are not inspired, they do provide insight into the views of some regarding the various settings. The title of Psalm 142 suggests that it was penned by David when he was in a cave. The cross reference is 1 Samuel 22:1. "So David departed from there and escaped to the cave of Adullam; and when his brothers and all his father's household heard of it, they went down there to him." This cave was one of the places in which David found himself after he fled from murderous King Saul. Psalm 57 carries a similar title.

The psalm doesn't require the title for it to be a meaningful source of comfort. If the title is appropriate, then it shows a man who only found a hiding place from one who was seeking his life. The cave did not provide him with a hiding place from the sorrow that burdened his soul.

Regardless of the exact setting of the Psalm, it emanated from a troubled heart.

The key aspect of this Psalm as a source of comfort is in the contrast presented in verses three and four. The writer looked to his fellow man for help but found none. He just wanted someone on whom he could rely. One who would be on another person's right hand would typically be his most trustworthy friend, his most dependable confidant. This confidant would provide the place of refuge or escape from the enemy. If this was indeed David writing this as he was on the run from Saul, then we can understand his anguish. Just before entering the cave, he had parted company with his best friend, Jonathan, whom he would never see alive again (1 Samuel 20:41-42). There was no longer anyone on earth to whom he could turn to escape the troubles he was facing.

On the other hand, God was there to give him the shelter from danger that he so intensely desired. There was no real help in man. If he wanted to escape his troubles and find refuge, he would find it only in God.

Application

When we face loss and grief, we too need a refuge. Sometimes we just need to get away. We need a break from all of the burdens that are mounting up. We need an escape. God is that escape. He is the source of strength, of constant spiritual energy. We need time with Him. We need time alone with Him.

Jesus knew the value of this time alone with God. Matthew 14:23 says, "After He had sent the crowds away, He went up on the mountain by Himself to pray; and when it was evening, He was there alone." Luke tells us, "It was at this time that He went off to the mountain to pray, and He spent the whole night in prayer to God" (Luke 6:12). With the agony of the cross and all that surrounded it looming before Him, Jesus went alone into the Garden of Gethsemane and poured out His heart to the Father (John 17).

The irony of this need to escape to our refuge and spend time with God alone in prayer and meditation of His Word is that well-meaning friends and family sometimes don't want to allow sufferers to have this time.

More than likely, they are simply concerned about the grieving person. Maybe they're afraid that the one who is grieving will harm himself or herself if left alone. Maybe they're concerned that the burden will be too great for the person to handle alone. Those dangers could indeed exist in some cases, but many times, those moments alone with God are the most significant in the comfort and even the spiritual growth of the one who is troubled.

The person who is dealing with loss and grief can be surrounded by family and friends and suddenly feel the need to get away for some quiet time. This is not a reflection on those who are trying to help. In fact, as odd as it may seem, that person may already be alone in his or her thoughts, even in a crowded room. Those who have experienced loss and grief know all about this. They know what it's like to feel isolated in a roomful of people, to hear voices but not words, to see shapes but not faces.

A grieving person should feel no shame in needing to get away. He or she should not feel the need to apologize for needing to get away, nor should anyone apologize for that person. That person just needs refuge. Yes, even in the midst of the closest of friends and family, the one who is grieving may need to break away and spend time with the only One who truly understands the intensity of the pain and who alone can provide the depth of comfort required.

God is the refuge for the troubled soul. Other Psalms echo this fact. "God is our refuge and strength, a very present help in trouble" (Psalm 46:1). "On God my salvation and my glory rest; the rock of my strength, my refuge is in God. Trust in Him at all times, O people; pour out your heart before Him; God is a refuge for us" (Psalm 62:7,8). "I will say to the Lord, My refuge and my fortress, my God, in whom I trust!" (Psalm 91:2). "But the Lord has been my stronghold, and my God the rock of my refuge" (Psalm 94:22).

Of course, one need not be alone to run to God for refuge. Prayer can be offered anytime and anywhere. Study of the Bible can take place anytime and anywhere. Times of worship with fellow Christians afford additional opportunities to go to God. Beyond this, however, the simple fact is that those who are experiencing grief due to a loss need time alone with God to be able to express their innermost feelings and deepest pain. Maybe there's even a special place to which one can go to have this time with God. A quiet room in the house, a special place that brings happy memories, or any number of locations could provide the place to which one can go when he or she needs that time alone in communion with the Lord.

God is the place of shelter for the troubled soul. He is the One to whom we can run to escape the burdens of life's difficulties and gain the strength we need to go back out and face them. "Cast your burden upon the Lord and He will sustain you; He will never allow the righteous to be shaken" (Psalm 55:22).

Key Takeaways from Chapter 21

- Time alone with God is an important part of recovering from loss and grief.
- The one who is grieving should feel no shame in needing to get away.
- God is the "escape" for those in grief when they need to get away for some quiet time.

Moments of Meditation

1. In what ways do reliable friends help us in our recovery from loss and grief?

_____

_____

_____

_____

2. Why did Jesus sometimes get away from the crowds and go off by Himself to pray?

_____

_____

_____

_____

_____

3. In what ways would time alone with God help you deal with your grief?

_____

_____

_____

_____

_____

4. In your grief, have you ever felt alone even though you were in a room filled with people? If so, how did you handle that feeling?

_____

_____

_____

_____

_____

5. What is the meaning of Psalm 55:22 ("Cast your burden upon the Lord and He will sustain you; He will never allow the righteous to be shaken.")?

_____

_____

_____

_____

_____

Create a quiet place where you can go to be alone to pray to God and meditate on His Word. You won't need to buy special furniture or decorations. It could be in your house, somewhere outside on your property, or some place that has special meaning to you. Inform your family of your quiet place and ask them to allow you the time that you need there to recover from your loss and grief. Let them know that they can come to you in case of an emergency, but other than that, you will need to be alone there.

Part Two
Individual Verses of Comfort

This part of the book offers a categorical listing of approximately 200 verses from the Psalms. Each category is phrased as an affirmation and is supported with at least one verse from Psalms. Any of these can be memorized and stored in your heart to ward off grief when it attacks. Moreover, learning them and even committing them to memory can go a long way toward helping you develop a positive mindset.

I Can Learn from My Troubles

- Psalm 119:67 – "Before I was afflicted I went astray, but now I keep Your word."

- Psalm 119:71 – "It is good for me that I was afflicted, that I may learn Your statutes."

I Can Have Confidence in God's Care

- Psalm 3:5 – "I lay down and slept; I awoke, for the LORD sustains me. "

- Psalm 4:8 – "In peace I will both lie down and sleep, For You alone, O LORD, make me to dwell in safety."

- Psalm 27:3 – "Though a host encamp against me, My heart will not fear; Though war arise against me, in *spite of* this I shall be confident."

God Always Blesses Me in Abundance

- Psalm 13:6 – "I will sing to the LORD, because He has dealt bountifully with me."

- Psalm 16:11 – "You will make known to me the path of life; in Your presence is fullness of joy; in Your right hand there are pleasures forever."

- Psalm 18:35 – "You have also given me the shield of Your salvation, and Your right hand upholds me; and Your gentleness makes me great."

- Psalm 25:6 – "Remember, O LORD, Your compassion and Your lovingkindnesses, for they have been from of old."

- Psalm 25:10 – "All the paths of the LORD are lovingkindness and truth to those who keep His covenant and His testimonies."

- Psalm 34:8-10 – "O taste and see that the LORD is good; how blessed is the man who takes refuge in Him! O fear the LORD, you His saints; for to those who fear Him there is no want. The young lions do lack and suffer hunger; but they who seek the LORD shall not be in want of any good thing."

- Psalm 36:7-9 – "How precious is Your lovingkindness, O God! And the children of men take refuge in the shadow of Your wings. They drink their fill of the abundance of Your house; and You give them to drink of the river of Your delights. For with You is the fountain of life; in Your light we see light."

- Psalm 37:16-17 – "Better is the little of the righteous than the abundance of many wicked. For the arms of the wicked will be broken, but the LORD sustains the righteous."

- Psalm 40:5 – "Many, O LORD my God, are the wonders which You have done, and Your thoughts toward us; there is none to compare with You. If I would declare and speak of them, they would be too numerous to count."

- Psalm 63:3 – "Because Your lovingkindness is better than life, my lips will praise You."

- Psalm 68:19 – "Blessed be the LORD, who daily bears our burden, the God *who* is our salvation."

- Psalm 84:11 – "For the LORD God is a sun and shield; the LORD gives grace and glory; no good thing does He withhold from those who walk uprightly."

- Psalm 86:15 – "But You, O LORD, are a God merciful and gracious, slow to anger and abundant in lovingkindness and truth."

- Psalm 100:4-5 – "Enter His gates with thanksgiving *and* His courts with praise. Give thanks to Him, bless His name. for the LORD is good; His lovingkindness is everlasting and His faithfulness to all generations."

- Psalm 103:8 – "The LORD is compassionate and gracious, slow to anger and abounding in lovingkindness."

- Psalm 107:8-9 – "Let them give thanks to the LORD for His lovingkindness, and for His wonders to the sons of men! For He has satisfied the thirsty soul, and the hungry soul He has filled with what is good."

- Psalm 116:5 – "Gracious is the LORD, and righteous; yes, our God is compassionate."

- Psalm 117:1-2 – "Praise the LORD, all nations; laud Him all peoples! For His lovingkindness is great toward us, and the truth of the Lord is everlasting. Praise the LORD."

- Psalm 118:29 – "Give thanks to the LORD, for He is good; for His lovingkindness is everlasting."

- Psalm 126:3 – "The LORD has done great things for us; we are glad."

- Psalm 146:5 – "How blessed is he whose help is the God of Jacob, whose hope is in the LORD his God."

God Can Deliver Me from My Troubles

- Psalm 17:7 – "Wondrously show Your lovingkindness, O Savior of those who take refuge at Your right hand from those who rise up *against them*."

- Psalm 25:15 – "My eyes are continually toward the LORD, for He will pluck my feet out of the net."

- Psalm 30:3 – "O LORD, You have brought up my soul from Sheol; You have kept me alive, that I would not go down to the pit."

- Psalm 34:4-6 – " I sought the LORD, and He answered me, and delivered me from all my fears. They looked to Him and were radiant, and their faces will never be ashamed. This poor man cried, and the LORD heard him and saved him out of all his troubles."

- Psalm 34:17-19 – "*The righteous* cry, and the LORD hears and delivers them out of all their troubles. The LORD is near to the brokenhearted and saves those who are crushed in spirit. Many are the afflictions of the righteous, but the LORD delivers him out of them all."

- Psalm 35:10 – "All my bones will say, "LORD, who is like You, who delivers the afflicted from him who is too strong for him, and the afflicted and the needy from him who robs him?"

- Psalm 40:1-2 – "I waited patiently for the LORD; and He inclined to me and heard my cry. He brought me up out of the pit of destruction, out of the miry clay, and He set my feet upon a rock making my footsteps firm."

- Psalm 66:12 – "You made men ride over our heads; we went through fire and through water, yet You brought us out into a *place of* abundance."

- Psalm 145:14 – "The LORD sustains all who fall and raises up all who are bowed down."

- Psalm 147:3 – "He heals the brokenhearted and binds up their wounds."

There Is No One Like Jehovah God

- Psalm 8:1 – "O LORD, our Lord, how majestic is Your name in all the earth, who have displayed Your splendor above the heavens!"

154

- Psalm 18:46 – "The LORD lives, and blessed be my rock; and exalted be the God of my salvation."

- Psalm 19:1-3 – "The heavens are telling of the glory of God; and their expanse is declaring the work of His hands. Day to day pours forth speech, and night to night reveals knowledge. There is no speech, nor are there words; their voice is not heard."

- Psalm 29:3-4 – "The voice of the LORD is upon the waters; the God of glory thunders, the LORD is over many waters. The voice of the LORD is powerful, the voice of the LORD is majestic."

- Psalm 29:10 – "The LORD sat *as King* at the flood; Yes, the LORD sits as King forever."

- Psalm 33:16-17 – "The king is not saved by a mighty army; a warrior is not delivered by great strength. A horse is a false hope for victory; nor does it deliver anyone by its great strength."

- Psalm 48:10 – "As is Your name, O God, so is Your praise to the ends of the earth; Your right hand is full of righteousness."

- Psalm 60:11 – "O give us help against the adversary, for deliverance by man is in vain."

- Psalm 71:19 – "For Your righteousness, O God, *reaches* to the heavens, You who have done great things; O God, who is like You? "

- Psalm 73:25 – "Whom have I in heaven *but You*? And besides You, I desire nothing on earth."

- Psalm 77:14 – "You are the God who works wonders; You have made known Your strength among the peoples."

- Psalm 90:1-2 – " Lord, You have been our dwelling place in all generations. Before the mountains were born or You gave birth to the earth and the world, even from everlasting to everlasting, You are God."

- Psalm 95:3-5 – "For the LORD is a great God and a great King above all gods, in whose hand are the depths of the earth, the peaks of the mountains are His also. The sea is His, for it was He who made it, and His hands formed the dry land."

- Psalm 96:4-6 – "For great is the LORD and greatly to be praised; He is to be feared above all gods. For all the gods of the peoples are idols, but the Lord made the heavens. Splendor and majesty are before Him, strength and beauty are in His sanctuary."

- Psalm 97:9 – "For You are the LORD Most High over all the earth; You are exalted far above all gods."

- Psalm 108:12 – "Oh give us help against the adversary, for deliverance by man is in vain."

- Psalm 113:2-6 – " Blessed be the name of the LORD from this time forth and forever. From the rising of the sun to its setting the name of the LORD is to be praised. The LORD is high above all nations; His glory is above the heavens. Who is like the LORD our God, who is enthroned on high, who humbles Himself to behold *the things that are* in heaven and in the earth? "

- Psalm 118:8-9 – "It is better to take refuge in the LORD than to trust in man. It is better to take refuge in the LORD than to trust in princes."

- Psalm 135:5 – "For I know that the LORD is great and that our Lord is above all gods."

- Psalm 147:5 – "Great is our Lord and abundant in strength; His understanding is infinite."

God Knows What's Happening in My Life

- Psalm 11:4 – "The LORD is in His holy temple; the LORD's throne is in heaven; His eyes behold, His eyelids test the sons of men."

- Psalm 24:1 – " The earth is the LORD's, and all it contains, the world, and those who dwell in it."

- Psalm 31:7-8 – "I will rejoice and be glad in Your lovingkindness, because You have seen my affliction; You have known the troubles of my soul, and You have not given me over into the hand of the enemy; You have set my feet in a large place."

- Psalm 40:17 – "Since I am afflicted and needy, let the Lord be mindful of me. You are my help and my deliverer; Do not delay, O my God."

God Will Never Fail Me

- Psalm 3:3 – " But You, O LORD, are a shield about me, my glory, and the One who lifts my head."

- Psalm 37:23-24 – "The steps of a man are established by the LORD, and He delights in his way. When he falls, he will not be hurled headlong, because the LORD is the One who holds his hand."

- Psalm 5:11-12 – "But let all who take refuge in You be glad, let them ever sing for joy; and may You shelter them, that those who love Your name may exult in You. For it is You who blesses the righteous man, O LORD, you surround him with favor as with a shield."

- Psalm 7:10 – "My shield is with God, who saves the upright in heart."

- Psalm 9:9-10 – "The LORD also will be a stronghold for the oppressed, a stronghold in times of trouble; and those who know Your name will put their trust in You, for You, O LORD, have not forsaken those who seek You."

- Psalm 17:8 – "Keep me as the apple of the eye; Hide me in the shadow of Your wings."

- Psalm 18:30 – "As for God, His way is blameless; the word of the LORD is tried; He is a shield to all who take refuge in Him."

- Psalm 27:5 – "For in the day of trouble He will conceal me in His tabernacle; in the secret place of His tent He will hide me; He will lift me up on a rock."

- Psalm 32:7 – "You are my hiding place; You preserve me from trouble; You surround me with songs of deliverance. Selah."

- Psalm 32:10 – "Many are the sorrows of the wicked, but he who trusts in the LORD, lovingkindness shall surround him."

- Psalm 33:20 – "Our soul waits for the LORD; He is our help and our shield."

- Psalm 48:14 – "For such is God, our God forever and ever; He will guide us until death."

- Psalm 57:1 – "Be gracious to me, O God, be gracious to me, for my soul takes refuge in You; and in the shadow of Your wings I will take refuge until destruction passes by."

- Psalm 62:1-2 – "My soul *waits* in silence for God only; from Him is my salvation. He only is my rock and my salvation, my stronghold; I shall not be greatly shaken."

- Psalm 62:6-7 – "He only is my rock and my salvation, my stronghold; I shall not be shaken. On God my salvation and my glory *rest*; the rock of my strength, my refuge is in God."

- Psalm 63:7 – "For You have been my help, and in the shadow of Your wings I sing for joy."

- Psalm 73:23-24 – "Nevertheless I am continually with You; You have taken hold of my right hand. With Your counsel You will guide me, and afterward receive me to glory."

- Psalm 94:17-18 – "If the LORD had not been my help, my soul would soon have dwelt in *the abode of* silence. If I should say,

'My foot has slipped,' Your lovingkindness, O LORD, will hold me up."

- Psalm 94:22 – "But the LORD has been my stronghold, and my God the rock of my refuge."

- Psalm 115:11 – "You who fear the LORD, trust in the LORD; He is their help and their shield."

- Psalm 116:7 – "Return to your rest, O my soul; for the Lord has dealt bountifully with you."

- Psalm 118:6 – "The LORD is for me; I will not fear; what can man do to me?"

- Psalm 121:2 – "My help comes from the LORD, who made heaven and earth."

- Psalm 121:5-8 – "The LORD is your keeper; the LORD is your shade on your right hand. The sun will not smite you by day, nor the moon by night. The LORD will protect you from all evil; He will keep your soul. The LORD will guard your going out and your coming in from this time forth and forever."

- Psalm 124:8 – "Our help is in the name of the LORD, who made heaven and earth."

- Psalm 140:7 – "O God the Lord, the strength of my salvation, You have covered my head in the day of battle."

God Hears the Prayers of the Righteous

- Psalm 3:4 – "I was crying to the LORD with my voice, and He answered me from His holy mountain. Selah."

- Psalm 4:3 – "But know that the LORD has set apart the godly man for Himself; the LORD hears when I call to Him."

- Psalm 6:9 – "The LORD has heard my supplication; the LORD receives my prayer."

- Psalm 22:24 – "For He has not despised nor abhorred the affliction of the afflicted; nor has He hidden His face from him; but when he cried to Him for help, He heard."

- Psalm 34:15 – "The eyes of the LORD are toward the righteous and His ears are *open* to their cry."

- Psalm 91:15 – "He will call upon me, and I will answer him: I will be with him in trouble; I will rescue him and honor him."

- Psalm 55:22 – "Cast your burden upon the LORD and he will sustain you; He will never allow the righteous to be shaken."

- Psalm 86:7 – "In the day of my trouble I shall call upon You, for You will answer me."

- Psalm 102:17 – "He has regarded the prayer of the destitute and has not despised their prayer."

- Psalm 118:5 – "From my distress I called upon the LORD; the LORD answered me and set me in a large place."

- Psalm 145:18 – "The Lord is near to all who call upon Him, to all who call upon Him in truth."

God Is My Strength

- Psalm 18:2 – "The LORD is my rock and my fortress and my deliverer, my God, my rock, in whom I take refuge; my shield and the horn of my salvation, my stronghold."

- Psalm 18:31 – "For who is God, but the LORD? And who is a rock, except our God?"

- Psalm 20:7 – "Some boast in chariots and some in horses, but we will boast in the name of the LORD, our God."

- Psalm 21:1 – "O LORD, in Your strength the king will be glad, and in Your salvation how greatly he will rejoice! "

- Psalm 27:1 – "The LORD is my light and my salvation; whom shall I fear? The Lord is the defense of my life; whom shall I dread?"

- Psalm 28:7 – "The LORD is my strength and my shield; my heart trusts in Him, and I am helped; therefore my heart exults, and with my song I shall thank him."

- Psalm 28:8 – "The LORD is their strength, and He is a saving defense to His anointed."

- Psalm 31:3 – "For You are my rock and my fortress; for your name's sake You will lead me and guide me."

- Psalm 37:39 – "But the salvation of the righteous is from the LORD; He is their strength in time of trouble."

- Psalm 46:1-3 – "God is our refuge and strength, a very present help in trouble. Therefore we will not fear, though the earth should change and though the mountains slip into the heart of the sea; though its waters roar and foam, though the mountains quake at its swelling pride. Selah."

- Psalm 73:26 – "My flesh and my heart may fail, but God is the strength of my heart and my portion forever."

- Psalm 59:9 – "*Because of* his strength I will watch for You, for God is my stronghold."

- Psalm 59:16-17 – "But as for me, I shall sing of Your strength; yes, I shall joyfully sing of Your lovingkindness in the morning, for You have been my stronghold and a refuge in the day of my distress. O my strength, I will sing praises to You; for God is my stronghold, the God who shows me lovingkindness.."

- Psalm 61:2-3 – "From the end of the earth I call to You when my heart is faint; lead me to the rock that is higher than I. For You have been a refuge for me, a tower of strength against the enemy."

- Psalm 71:16 – "I will come with the mighty deeds of the Lord GOD; I will make mention of Your righteousness, Yours alone."

- Psalm 89:8 – "O LORD God of hosts, who is like You, O mighty LORD? Your faithfulness also surrounds You?"

- Psalm 89:13 – "You have a strong arm; Your hand is mighty, Your right hand is exalted."

- Psalm 118:14 – "The LORD is my strength and song, and He has become my salvation."

I Can Rely on God's Word

- Psalm 12:6 – "The words of the LORD are pure words; as silver tried in a furnace on the earth, refined seven times."

- Psalm 19:7-8 – "The law of the LORD is perfect, restoring the soul; the testimony of the LORD is sure, making wise the simple. The precepts of the LORD are right, rejoicing the heart; The commandment of the LORD is pure, enlightening the eyes."

- Psalm 25:5 – "Lead me in your truth and teach me, for You are the God of my salvation; for You I wait all the day."

- Psalm 33:4 – "For the word of the LORD is upright, and all his work is *done* in faithfulness."

- Psalm 119:28 – "My soul weeps because of grief, strengthen me according to Your word."

- Psalm 119:49-50 – "Remember the word to Your servant, in which you have made me hope. This is my comfort in my affliction, that Your word has revived me."

- Psalm 119:92-93 – "If Your law had not been my delight, then I would have perished in my affliction. I will never forget Your precepts, for by them You have revived me."

- Psalm 119:105 – "Your word is a lamp to my feet and a light to my path."

- Psalm 119:114 – "You are my hiding place and my shield; I wait for your word."

- Psalm 119:140 – "Your word is very pure, therefore your servant loves it."

- Psalm 119:142-143 – "Your righteousness is an everlasting righteousness, and Your law is truth. Trouble and anguish have come upon me, *yet* Your commandments are my delight."

- Psalm 119:165 – "Those who love Your law have great peace, and nothing causes them to stumble."

As Long as I Walk with God, I Will Always Have Hope

- Psalm 31:24 – "Be strong and let your heart take courage, all you who hope in the LORD."

- Psalm 38:15 – "For I hope in You, O LORD; You will answer, O Lord my God."

- Psalm 42:5 – "Why are you in despair, O my soul? and why have you become disturbed within me? Hope in God, for I shall again praise Him for the help of His presence."

- Psalm 42:11 – "Why are you in despair, O my soul? And why have you become disturbed within me? Hope in God, for I shall yet praise Him, the help of my countenance and my God."

- Psalm 43:5 – "Why are you in despair, O my soul? And why are you disturbed within me? Hope in God, for I shall again praise Him, the help of my countenance and my God."

- Psalm 71:14 – "But as for me, I will hope continually, and will praise You yet more and more."

My Life Would Be Empty Without God

- Psalm 39:4-5 – "LORD, make me to know my end and what is the extent of my days; let me know how transient I am. Behold, You have made my days as handbreadths, and my lifetime as nothing in Your sight; surely every man at his best is a mere breath. Selah."

I Can Develop Patience Through My Troubles

- Psalm 27:14 – "Wait for the LORD; be strong and let your heart take courage; yes, wait for the LORD."

- Psalm 37:7-9 – "Rest in the LORD and wait patiently for Him; do not fret because of him who prospers in his way, because of the man who carries out wicked schemes. Cease from anger and forsake wrath; do not fret; *it leads* only to evildoing. For evildoers will be cut off, but those who wait for the LORD, they will inherit the land."

- Psalm 46:10 – "Cease *striving* and know that I am God; I will be exalted among the nations, I will be exalted in the earth."

- Psalm 62:5 – "My soul, wait in silence for God only, for my hope is from Him."

My Mind Can Be at Ease

- Psalm 94:19 – "When my anxious thoughts multiply within me, Your consolations delight my soul."

In God I Have Found a Friend I Can Trust

- Psalm 56:3-4 – "When I am afraid, I will put my trust in You. In God, whose word I praise, in God I have put my trust; I shall not be afraid. What can mere man do to me?"

- Psalm 56:11 – "In God I have put my trust, I shall not be afraid. What man can do to me?"

- Psalm 57:1 – "Be gracious to me, O God, be gracious to me, for my soul takes refuge in You; and in the shadow of Your wings I will take refuge until destruction passes by."

- Psalm 62:8 – "Trust in Him at all times, O people; pour out your heart before Him: God is a refuge for us. Selah."

- Psalm 71:5 – "For You are my hope, O Lord God, *You are* my confidence from my youth."

I Can Be Victorious Over All of Life's Troubles

- Psalm 41:11 – "By this I know that You are pleased with me, because my enemy does not shout in triumph over me."

- Psalm 64:10 – "The righteous man will be glad in the LORD and will take refuge in Him; and all the upright in heart will glory."

- Psalm 92:12-15 – "The righteous man will flourish like the palm tree, he will grow like a cedar in Lebanon. Planted in the house of the LORD, they will flourish in the courts of our God. They will still yield fruit in old age; they shall be full of sap and very green, to declare that the LORD is upright; *He is* my rock, and there is no unrighteousness in Him."

- Psalm 116:15 – "Precious in the sight of the Lord is the death of His godly ones."

- Psalm 138:7 – "Though I walk in the midst of trouble, You will revive me; You will stretch forth Your hand against the wrath of my enemies, and Your right hand will save me."

The Lord Is My Shepherd

- Psalm 23:1-6 – "The LORD is my shepherd, I shall not want. He makes me lie down in green pastures; He leads me beside quiet waters. He restores my soul; He guides me in the paths of righteousness for His name's sake. Even though I walk through the valley of the shadow of death, I fear no evil, for You are with me; Your rod and Your staff, they comfort me. You prepare a table before me in the presence of my enemies; You have anointed my head with oil; My cup overflows. Surely goodness and lovingkindness will follow me all the days of my life, and I will dwell in the house of the LORD forever."

- Psalm 79:13 – "So we Your people and the sheep of Your pasture will give thanks to you forever; To all generations we will tell of Your praise."

- Psalm 100:3 – "Know that the LORD Himself is God; It is He who has made us, and not we ourselves; *we are* His people and the sheep of His pasture."

Part Three
Sitting in the Lap of God

(Note: The following pages contain excerpts from a blog that Shannon and I maintained in the closing weeks of her life. It was entitled, "A Couple Conquers Cancer." She added her comments as she was able, sometimes dictating them to me. Several thousand people visited the blog during this time, some on numerous occasions. It was a great way for us to keep friends and family apprised of Shannon's condition. It was also a great outlet for dealing with the challenges we were facing. – M.G.)

February 25
Conquering, Not Just Coping

The idea for this site started with a focus on how we as a married couple have been coping with cancer. When I looked up the word, "coping" and found that it means, "to struggle or deal, esp. on fairly even terms or with some degree of success," I felt that the word was so bland. To me, the idea of coping with something means you're putting up with it. Well, I don't want to put up with cancer. I want to beat it into submission. I want to control it, not allow it to control me. In short, I want to conquer it.

The Key to Success (from Shannon)

The key to managing a challenge such as this is to stick together. There is no way I could possibly face the many doctor visits, pokes, prods, hospital stays, chemotherapy, and other trappings of cancer without a strong support system. That support begins with my husband of 30 years, who has never wavered in his love and strength. I draw from that strength to help me through each day.

February 26
"We"?

A lot of times I'll talk about how "we" are going through this. That may sound kind of strange. After all, Shannon is the one with the disease. I can't feel the pain she's experiencing, but I do feel pain. It just hurts in a different way. The emotional strain is the most challenging and from time to time that spills over into some physical pain. It's not really "sympathy pains" like a husband gets during his wife's labor. It's real pain. Casting this stress on God in prayer, as He invites us to in 1 Peter 5:7, is my outlet for relief. When one is caring for a spouse with an illness, he or she needs to acknowledge the strain and take the necessary actions to deal with it so that they can have the physical strength to be there when their spouse needs them.

February 27
Day One

Time now to fill in some blanks. May 27 was the day we first heard the word "cancer" and Shannon's name used in the same sentence. The two of us were alone in the car when she told me. I took the news calmly. My immediate reaction was to try to reassure her that everything would be okay. I believed that and, in fact, I still do.

Half an hour later I was breaking the news to our children. What caused that word to stick in my throat and be held back by tears at that point I'm not sure I'll ever know. Maybe it was a rush of memories of all of the years Shannon and I had had together with our children; maybe it was the mistaken notion that a diagnosis of cancer was an immediate death sentence; maybe it was looking into the eyes of my children and feeling the pain that I knew they would feel in just a few moments when the word finally came out of my mouth; maybe it was just having to say the word, "cancer." Whatever the cause, the word did not come easily.

Tears and hugs and reassurances came next, followed by frank talk of a practical plan for dealing with our new challenge. Our routine would be interrupted. There would be hospital stays forthcoming, treatments to take, medical equipment to which we would need to get accustomed. In effect, multiple changes were coming and could not be stopped.

When cancer comes, it doesn't sneak in gradually. It rushes in like a flood, bringing with it previously untouched emotions, untold challenges, and an uncertain outcome.

February 28
The Story Continues

Last July, we spent a few days (or years, depending on your perspective) at a hospital about an hour away. The surgery was successful, but we were still facing cancer. By this time, we were both thinking, "When is this nightmare going to be over?" Other than having four babies, Shannon had never had a hospital stay and I've never been an overnight patient in a hospital at any time in my life.

One thing you'd better learn in a hospital is patience, and you'd better learn it in a hurry. It's not anything like being at home. You can't run down to the refrigerator and grab a snack. Privacy is unheard of (and, by the way, 70% of the people who pass by an open hospital room door look in; 100% of those who look in think it's strange when the room's occupant waves at them). Obviously, the sleeping arrangements are different, as are the smells, the sounds, and even the television. It's a different world and BOTH the patient and spouse have to adapt.

Routines (from Shannon)

The day your diagnosis is listed as "cancer" is a day that is not easily forgotten. It seems as if your life is separated by a gulf; the days that happened before cancer, and then the days after. The challenge of fighting this disease permeates every pore, invades every thought.

It is easy to become overwhelmed by the everyday changes. New medications must be taken, often to a confusing level of intricacy. Equipment might be needed, such as oxygen machinery or special monitoring devices. There are feelings of isolation, frustration, and exhaustion.

169

Eventually, one becomes familiar with what was once totally alien. The sound of the oxygen machine, while still loud, is now a familiar sound. The wires and tubes are organized, and the routine is set. The internet and the telephone help ward away isolation while big windows bring in lots of sunshine and views of the outside world to bring variety to the day.

And then you can fight....and fight...and fight. Our motto has become, "Fight every day; enjoy every moment!"

March 1
The Next Chapter

The phrase, "the dog days of summer" took on a new meaning for us in August of last year. On August 8, Shannon was at home and having difficulty breathing. I was going to drive her to the emergency room, but when she could barely walk as far as the living room, we decided to call the ambulance. Later we would discover that the cancer had spread to her lungs and had caused a hole in one of them that had it functioning at only 10% of its capacity. While in surgery, a cancer-induced hole developed in the other lung. Thus began a string of 25 days in the hospital, interrupted by only a few days off back at home.

It was during this time that I experienced what was, without a doubt, the lowest point of my life. One day, struggling for a breath, Shannon said to me, "Take care of the kids." I knew her medications might be affecting her mood, but still, it felt like she was giving up. All I remember saying is, "I refuse to believe you're going to die from this. We will not lose." She had demonstrated such a strong will to that point; now she needed to borrow some of my determination. It was only fair that I lend it. After all, she had already given me so much of hers.

March 3
Finishing Up Last Year

After our August/mid-September hospital ordeal, we fell into sort of a routine back at home. Granted, it was a routine different from anything we had ever experienced in our lives, but it was a routine, nonetheless. There were still rough days, but the news that the chemotherapy was making a difference helped us deal with those. As the holidays approached, we looked forward to the family being together. Even when December brought the news that this treatment had stopped working and that we would have to move on to another after the first of the year, we were still excited about the holidays. They gave us something to look forward to. We've found that to be important. Whether these things are large (the family coming together, going on a short trip) or small (bringing home a movie to watch together, cooking a favorite meal), the anticipation of positive events has helped us deal with the down times.

March 6
Off Schedule

I'll admit to being "schedule happy." I like everything to be organized, in its proper place and just so. But cancer has its own schedule. For instance, while I had planned for the last few days to update the history of our encounter with this illness, one of the offshoots of the cancer decided to attack Shannon again, bringing her back to the hospital. Ideally, we were going to post here daily, each one of us playing off the other in our writing. She just hasn't had the strength and is barely able to talk, much less write.

Dealing with cancer requires flexibility. You go where you need to go and change what you need to change in order to accommodate the unexpected. Basically, the whole experience is filled with unexpected twists and turns. While learning from those who have gone through this is helpful, no two experiences are exactly alike. Learn what you can from what others have to say, but don't be frustrated if things don't happen on the same timetable as it did for them.

March 7
Up to Date

To finish the timeline of our experience, I don't recall ever looking forward to a new year more than I looked forward to this one. Last year had brought some other challenges in addition to the cancer so the prospect of a fresh start was pleasant. It was another of those "things to look forward to" that we tried to keep in front of us to help us keep going.

For the first six weeks of this year, we went through the weekly treatment regimen, only briefly interrupted by a visit to the emergency room, not really knowing if any progress was being made. A scan on February 22 told us that, in fact, no progress had been made, and the cancer was worsening. In addition, the scan revealed the lungs were again collapsing. A few hours after the scan, we were again in the hospital and stayed for five days, only to come back again four days later with recurring issues related to the lungs as well as pneumonia that had developed.

So here we are in our third-floor condo and now you are up to date. Several words come to mind in summarizing the past nine and a half months, among which are: unique, challenging, frightening, faith-building. However, through it all I can say that I can't think of a time when we lost hope. We've never really faced any long-term challenges in our lives. This is a first. All those years of studying God's inspired Word (the Bible) and committing it to heart and mind have, I'm convinced, built a wall around us that is protecting us from despair and doubt.

March 8
Riding the Roller Coaster

Roller coasters have never been a favorite of mine. I prefer to keep my stomach in one location. Dealing with cancer is a roller coaster ride of epic proportions. One day you're riding high when things seem to be going well. On another day you've been hurtled down literally into "the valley of the shadow of death," wondering if this is the last time you'll get to hold your spouse and see her sweet face this side of eternity. On still another day, everything seems normal, like it was in the pre-cancer days. For me, an important factor in dealing with this is to maintain an even keel. Don't panic in the valleys. Don't become unrealistic at the peaks. Stay steady and enjoy the time you have with your loved one, caressing every moment you have together as if it were the last.

(Actually, why should we wait for a long-term illness to make us appreciate life's precious moments?)

The last two days have been good ones as we wait for the pneumonia to go away while anticipating surgical repair of Shannon's lungs. With the completion of these two steps, we can move on to the next treatment in hopes that this will be the one that sends the cancer into remission.

March 10
Peace That Passes All Understanding

So far, so good on today's surgery. The pneumonia skirmish and now the lung skirmish still occupy us and are keeping us from fighting the bigger battle of cancer. Thankfully, we're beating back these enemies, so it is with high hopes that we prepare to take on the major adversary within the next week to ten days.

With each challenge we've faced we have seen Bible verses come to life. Verses such as Philippians 4:6-7 (I'm going to make you get your Bible and look those up) have always been meaningful and powerful because the Bible is God's living Word (Hebrews 4:12), but here, in a surgery pre-op room, I actually see the peace that passes all understanding in Shannon's eyes. This is not a tumultuous time for either of us. Instead, it's an opportunity for us to enjoy God's blessings.

March 13
A Little Courtesy

Even though we're in that "hurry up and wait" mode, the last couple of days have been peaceful. Shannon is eating well, breathing well and, aside from the napping that comes along with the pain medication, is in many ways back to herself. I knew things were bad a week or so ago when she said she didn't want any chocolate. Thankfully, she's eaten everything chocolate I've brought to her lately.

We've known the value of courtesy from our youth. Having spent little time in the hospital, I'm nonetheless aware of the challenges and pressures faced by the staff. Some time ago I remember reading something that suggested the hospital staff appreciates "please" and "thank you." It may not be much, but we've tried to use those words as often as possible during our stays. The doctors, nurses and the rest of the crew put in a lot of work. We've struck up conversations with just about all of them. It seems that just a little common courtesy from a patient might make their jobs more enjoyable.

March 16
Up for a Bit of Air (from Shannon)

The past week has been a blur of procedures and fevers and medications. I'm feeling better today and am happy to be enjoying this lovely day.

I am so blessed with family and friends, who encourage me to keep fighting. I will!

March 22
Home Again

Last Wednesday, all things were "go" for leaving the hospital. I had gone to pick up a prescription, our boys were waiting in the hallway outside of Shannon's room, and she was inside preparing to dress, sign discharge papers, and leave. Suddenly she lost a significant amount of blood and passed out. The nurses revived her, but by the next morning she was in surgery again, this time in an effort to stop the incessant bleeding she has been experiencing for so many months. A day or two prior to all of this we thought again that we might be going home but a very dangerous attack came then as well and, thankfully, soon went. When Friday came and they released us, we were watching every step to make sure this time our departure would come to pass. Her many continuous days in bed weakened her leg muscles but her determination had her quickly adjusting and she is now getting around with the help of a walker. She is eating and resting well, and we look forward to being able to once again attack the source of all of this, the cancer.

The Psalmist wrote, "I will give thanks to You, for I am fearfully and wonderfully made..." (Psalm 139:14). The complexity of the human body has never been so evident to me as it is now. Our bodies are so intricate that, while the vast majority of our muscles, cells, etc. are working properly, one tiny, afflicted area can stop us in our tracks. That's not always bad. In this case, had we gotten home on Wednesday and had Shannon lost the blood and passed out at home instead of in the hospital, the results could have been much worse. At the time we were disappointed that we were not going home, but the cause of our disappointment actually turned out to be a blessing. I may sound like my needle is stuck in a groove (that's "record" talk for you younger folks) but you really don't want to get too bound up in a schedule when dealing with cancer. Circumstances can change in an instant.

March 23
Normal (from Shannon)

The definition of "normal" changes often during this type of challenge. Normal, a year ago, meant shopping trips, visits with friends, and lots of church activities. Normal, today, means taking meds, resting, visiting assorted doctors, and rebuilding strength.

It's important to me to have something that feels really "Normal". My online classes have been my "normal" thing to do. It takes me away from the IVs, the strong medicines, and the odd smells that come with this.

I must admit, I'm impatient. I want to be outside, smelling those hyacinths and feeling the fresh air. I want to visit with friends and attend every church activity possible. These things will come; I must be patient. In the meantime, redefining normal is a daily process.

March 25
Another Bend in the Road

It's been such a joy to be home. Tomorrow, we will make our way back to the hospital for another surgery. We're in that vicious cycle of trying to fight the cancer but being prohibited by other complications that are being caused by the cancer. The apostle Paul wrote, "We are afflicted in every way, but not crushed; perplexed, but not despairing" (2 Corinthians 4:8). The battle is getting tougher. How anyone can face death without the faith that comes from God's written Word is hard to imagine. The Bible gives us plenty of examples of men and women of faith. It's my privilege to be able to see a living example of faith in Shannon every day.

March 27
A Time for Appreciation

Today we were told that the surgery we were expecting to have is not necessary at this time. On Tuesday we expect to have the other chest tube removed. We're thankful for every positive step. We're trying to make sure that we don't spend so much time asking that we forget to give thanks.

March 31
I Don't Know What to Say

Yesterday, Shannon had a radiation treatment, its purpose being to lessen and hopefully eliminate her blood loss. Today brings with it the typical side effects, but her temperature has been normal for two days, so that good news offsets the harshness of the radiation. She says she's not in pain, just weak. She always has enough strength for a sweet smile when I need one though. I've burned that look into my mind for the past 31 years that we've known each other and carry it with me.

Many times, people don't know what to say to folks in a situation like ours. A feeling of inadequacy gnaws at them as they avoid saying anything for fear of saying the wrong thing. That lack of communication then turns to guilt for not talking at all to the sufferers. It's a vicious cycle. If you've ever had this happen to you, allow me to help you out. Say, "I'm sorry," "I'm thinking of you and praying for you," "I love you," "I want you to know how much you mean to me." These are simple, few-word statements. After saying the one or ones of your choosing, sit back and listen. Don't probe. Just listen. Let that person lead the conversation. Whether you're talking by phone or in person, you don't have to keep the conversation going for a long time. Just knowing that they are in someone's heart is sufficient for most people dealing with a critical illness.

April 2
Two Steps Ahead, A Brief Step Back

For the first time since last August, Shannon is breathing without the aid of an oxygen machine or tank. The work that was done in repairing her lungs was apparently successful. The cancer had traveled there through lymph nodes and caused damage. The tumors continue to grow in the lungs but we're hoping to get another chemotherapy treatment to see if it can help.

We're still in the hospital due to Shannon's persistent fever. It's just a couple or a few degrees over normal, but when we're talking about body temperature, that small range can be a huge factor in one's health. Sometimes it's the seemingly tiniest things that can slow you down. Thankfully, there have been more positives than negatives today.

April 3
Making the Hard Choices

Throughout our battle with this illness, we've found ourselves faced with challenging choices. None was more challenging than today. When we learned earlier in the week that our daughter, Whitney, and grandson, Daniel, would be coming today for a week's visit, we set our hearts on getting home so that we could spend time with them. Based on the fever that just doesn't want to go away, the doctors informed us that they had different plans if we still wanted to try to get a chemotherapy treatment and take advantage of the 20-30% chance they say we have of this treatment working. They felt that the best way to be prepared for the treatment would be for Shannon to be under constant care in the hospital. Home health care would be available if we went home, but of course, it would not be available 24/7 like it is in the hospital.

So here we were, on one hand wanting to spend quality time with our family members who had flown halfway across the country, and on the other hand wanting to at least get a shot at the treatment that we have not been able to take due to one reason or another for so many months. If the treatment has such a small chance of being effective, would it be best to just go on home and enjoy the family in a more familiar environment? If the treatment has any chance at all of being effective, no matter how slim that chance may be, would it be best to stay in the hospital, sacrificing that week of family time for the hope of having many more weeks of family time in the future?

We opted for the prolonged stay in the hospital. Since the element of risk is evident on all sides, we decided to go the route of doing whatever we can to get to the treatment and hope and pray that the 20-30% chance is enough. Talking things out with one another and with the doctors seems to be key to making the hard choices.

April 4
Sometimes the Choices Are Made for You

Yesterday's difficult decision turned into a non-decision today as the doctors informed us that the cancer is now untreatable. While a chemotherapy treatment could still be an option, the scans show that the tumors are growing so rapidly that a treatment would virtually be of no effect and would in fact make Shannon feel worse.

So now we go home to familiar surroundings, hoping to make her comfortable. She's not in pain, just getting weaker. She's also not afraid. This is "the valley of the shadow of death" of which the Psalmist wrote in Psalm 23:4. We both know the Shepherd of this Psalm and right now we are walking beside Him, hand in hand. Soon, I'll need to let go, but Shannon will continue her walk through the valley, not alone, but in the presence of the One who can safely lead her home.

April 5
From Shannon

Despite the disappointment of knowing that medical treatment is no longer effective, I am thankful. I am thankful for the many friends who have expressed their love and concern for me, for my family who has been so supportive through this ordeal and particularly, I am thankful for my husband who has been my strength.

God is good. I know He will take care of me, and I know He will take care of those I leave behind.

April 6
Just Another Ordinary, Everyday Love Story - Part 1

For over 30 years, I have been married to my best friend. Occasionally, someone will comment on the longevity of our relationship and wonder how we've done it. If you'll indulge me a little meandering down memory lane, I'd like to share how Shannon and I got to this point in our lives where, as a single-minded force, we have been able to stare down cancer and conquer it. (Yes, conquer it. Even though it will eventually claim Shannon's life, cancer has not defeated us. If its intention was to discourage us and cause us to grow apart due to the stress and strain it causes, it has failed miserably. We have only become stronger and closer as a result of this.)

When we first met at fine arts camp in Henderson, TN in 1978, we didn't like each other very much. I was the new kid in town, and she thought I was a dumb athlete (she always has been good at judging character). She was very sure of herself, had been a part of that group for a couple of years, and held some leadership positions. I thought she was snooty. A week or so later, in my first semester at Freed-Hardeman University, I had pretty much forgotten about her, choosing instead to focus on getting acquainted with other people at the school as well as my new surroundings.

Sometime into the semester the drama department was holding auditions for "The Music Man." I tried out and won a small role. You can probably imagine who the student director was - Shannon. At that point, our opinions of each other had not changed, but as days of rehearsals passed, I began to notice something about her. I again saw that self-assurance, but this time in a different light. I saw it even in the face of a bunch of male teenage cast members who sometimes weren't very respectful of their young, female leader. I also saw an interest in and concern for other people. There was something there that I had never really seen before in a young lady and suddenly I wanted to get to know her better.

I asked her out and, thankfully, she agreed to go with me to dinner at The Old Country Store in Jackson, TN and then to Bible class afterward.

It was a memorable evening for me. Does that mean I remember all the details? Well, I recall where we sat, but if you ask me what I ate and what she ate, forget about it. Regarding the meal itself, suffice it to say that we ate food, got full, I paid the check, and we left. But this person for whom I previously had little regard had now captured my thoughts, and, as I would soon find out, my heart.

More to come...

April 7
Shannon's Turn

Coming home has been bittersweet. While I am thrilled to be back in familiar surroundings and away from the sterile atmosphere of the hospital, I know that this will be the last place on earth I will live. However, doesn't it seem more appropriate to go from the home that has given me joy and pleasure for so many years directly into the home for which I've waited all my life?

I will be leaving one set of loving hands to go to another. I am not afraid, I'm in no pain, and I'm thankful to still have a clear enough brain to be able to enjoy my family. I love you all.

Just Another Ordinary, Everyday Love Story - Part 2

I am the world's fastest shopper. When I see what I like, I get it. I've always been that way. So maybe it shouldn't come as a surprise that after our first date and six more days of seeing and getting to know Shannon, I asked her to marry me. That's right, it took me a whole week to muster the courage to ask her to be my wife. When people say that you'll "just know" when you find the right one, they are right, at least in my case. A little more than a year later, we were married. Shannon was dressed in a beautiful white gown that she had made on the sewing machine I had bought her for her birthday. Not being a person who readily shows his emotions, I nonetheless cried throughout the ceremony, not so much out of nervousness as out of gratitude for and amazement at the gift God had given me.

When I say that ours is just another ordinary, everyday love story, I mean just that. Our life together has had very little drama. We have never been on the brink of marital collapse. We have both been faithful to each other and to the vows we made in the sight of God. Our children have been outstanding and continue to faithfully serve God as Christians. Basically, if I were to write our story in a book, I probably couldn't pay people to take the copies. Our life is just not "Hollywood" enough.

In spite of how mundane our life might appear to some, it has been filled with constant open communication, mutual respect, and love for one another and for God. Just as a person is not fully grown on the day of his birth, a marriage is not fully grown right after the "I Do's" are said. To use another metaphor, marriage is a house constantly under construction, never completed until one of the spouses leaves this life.

Now we come to this, the final chapter of our story. Each challenge we've faced, each prayer we've prayed, each Bible verse we've read, each midnight heart-to-heart, each tear and each success we've experienced over 30+ years have made this past year and its many challenges seem, as the apostle Paul said, like a "light affliction" (2 Corinthians 4:17). To get to this point, we really haven't done anything that any other married couple can't themselves do. Devotion to God and commitment to one another as husband and wife are attainable by all.

April 9
When Love Takes Over

When we learned that Shannon's cancer was untreatable, we had yet another decision to make. Should we stay in the hospital with 24/7 care or go home with the assistance of hospice? Frankly, to me, it was never in question that we would go home. Who doesn't want to be home? However, Shannon was concerned that she would be a burden. I imagine that this is not uncommon among those in her situation and that it can become a nagging feeling, despite constant reassurances to the contrary.

Since being home, I've learned some valuable new skills as a caregiver. I've also developed a heightened appreciation for all those men and women who tended to Shannon in the hospital. Whether they were administering medicine, changing sheets, or whatever, those who give their lives to serving in medical care are wonderful people. No job that they do is unimportant.

The role that I have now assumed has allowed me to plumb the depths of my love for Shannon and, as I have done so, I find that it is as deep as I always felt it was. None of the tasks I now do for her is burdensome in the least. I'm sure the most difficult task will be that of finally letting her go, although I'll never let her out of my heart.

April 10
Planning Ahead

Among the difficult tasks I've encountered in the past week is that of preparing for my life without Shannon. Like a lot of people, we've planned for our deaths with wills, insurance, etc., but in the planning stages, death seems so far away. There's a considerable difference between the preparation for and the practical application of the deeds and events surrounding the death of one's spouse. The former is "way off in the distance" (or so we think), while the latter is staring you right in the face.

For over 30 years I've relied on Shannon to help me organize the many facets of our life together. Ironically, I am now relying on her to help me organize my life without her. Whether I'm asking her where something is or how to do something that she had typically done, I'm thankful for her patient answers. I'm also thankful to know that, even though there will be a major void in my life after she's gone, the example she set in life will continue to influence me as I'm sure it will those whose lives she has touched.

Enjoying the Moments

Over the 31+ years that we have known each other, Shannon and I have written memories that would fill a library full of books. We've never been ones to sit around and dwell on the past though. Sure, we've taken the pictures and filmed the significant events, but we rarely sit down and relive those memories. I guess it's because we're too busy in the present making more memories.

Interestingly enough, even now we're continuing this pattern. While we've been admiring old family photos and home movies from time to time since coming home, we still spend her waking minutes talking about our family as they are now, our friends, current events, and God's faithfulness to us during this time. In short, we seem to be enjoying the moments we have together just as we always have without an overemphasis on the past or the future. Sometimes it's difficult to look into her eyes and not project myself into my future without her, but the effort to save that for my "private time" is well worth it and allows me to get the most out of this time that we have together.

April 12
Appropriate Scriptures

Shannon continues to battle bravely each day, but she is getting weaker as the doctors said she would. She has minimal pain, but other than the occasional Tylenol to ease her fevers, she takes no pain medication. She speaks openly to me of what is going on inside her, and though it's difficult to hear, I know I need to be aware of it so that I can be the most help to her.

Several people who have contacted us have cited the qualities of the virtuous woman of Proverbs 31 as an appropriate description of Shannon's life. I feel the same way, considering verse 30 to be especially accurate. "Charm is deceitful and beauty is vain, but a woman who fears the Lord, she shall be praised." In this case, I have been triply blessed in that while I found a lady who fears the Lord, I also know her to be charming and beautiful.

Another section of God's Word that comes to mind when I think of Shannon is Acts 9:36-41 where we read of Tabitha, also called Dorcas. Read those verses for yourself, especially verse 39, and see if you don't picture in your mind's eye the countless number of women who could stand around Shannon, holding out garments that she made or that she helped others make.

The Divinely inspired verse that really stands out to me is the one that I know will apply to her for years after her passing. The Divinely inspired writer told of Abel's righteousness, saying, "though he is dead, he still speaks" (Hebrews 11:4). I am confident that Shannon will live on in the hearts of those she touched through sewing, through her Bible class teaching, through her loyal friendship, and through her Christ-like example. Even now she shares smiles with those who see her and talk to her. I believe all who know her will carry a piece of her in their hearts and will benefit greatly as a result.

April 13
My Energizer Bunny

Here's your word for the day: Indomitable. Look it up, and if you don't see a picture of Shannon next to the definition then you have a faulty dictionary.

As visitors have come by in the last week, some have talked about items that they are sewing or quilting. As you might have guessed, somewhere in those conversations, Shannon has been sharing tips to help those folks complete their projects. The apostle Paul quoted Jesus as saying, "It is more blessed to give than to receive" (Acts 20:35). I have to smile as I watch Shannon continuing to give of herself, even in her weakened condition.

She's having a good day and has eaten more today than she has in several days. As always, we enjoy these days and are thankful for them.

April 15
Going Against the Grain

As expected, Shannon is sleeping more. We seem to have the right mix of medications going so when she's awake she is alert. She's having some pain, but we're able to lessen it before it gets too severe.

I'll have to admit that I'm blazing some new trails for myself here. In the past, whenever Shannon got sick, I knew my job was to make sure she got what she needed so that she would get back to full health. Now, because she is not expected to recover, I can't do anything to help her get better. I can only make her comfortable and try to ease her pain. Initially, it was difficult to accept this because one's basic nature is to help an ill loved one recover. Now that I have a better understanding of my role, I realize that by seeing to her comfort, I am helping her as much as I ever have.

April 16
Talk About Priceless

Remember the "priceless" credit card commercials? Glancing over at Shannon to discover that she has been gazing at me and smiling; catching that gleam in her eye that makes my heart melt; sharing a look that only those who have ever truly been in love can understand - now that's priceless.

She's had another good day today, eating well, resting well, and enjoying occasional, brief visits. I'm glad we decided to come home and I'm thankful for our friends and family who have helped make this time so pleasurable. They're the best.

April 17
Celebrate the Simple Pleasures

By her actions, Shannon reminds me on a daily basis of the importance of the little things in life. She was so excited the other day because the swelling in her feet had gone down and she could move her toes. Today, it was biscuits, gravy, and sausage from Ross's Diner that brightened her morning. You ought to see her light up when she gets a piece of fresh fruit. For so many months during the chemotherapy, she wasn't allowed to have it and now with every bite it seems as though she's tasting it for the first time.

In the Sermon on the Mount, Jesus told His audience to "look at the birds of the air" and "observe how the lilies of the field grow" to learn a lesson about God's care for His people (Matthew 6:26, 28). These are just simple, everyday things, but like so many other facets of God's creation, they can elicit joy and appreciation in the hearts of those who are willing to slow down for a moment or two and take a look at them.

Shannon has had another good day today and continues to share her smiles.

April 18
Homecoming

This evening at 8:59 p.m. Eastern time, Shannon went home to be with the Lord. She was not in any pain and was surrounded by loved ones. As you would expect of her if you knew her, her final words were those of encouragement, telling us how much she loved us and how happy her life had been.

Shannon's life was one well-lived. With faith in God and love for others, she touched so many people across the globe. It was my blessed privilege to be her husband since December 30, 1979. I can't begin to imagine what my life would have been without her. She made my time here so joyful. There wasn't any challenge that we weren't able to overcome together, including this one.

The title of this site is "A Couple Conquers Cancer." As a faithful Christian, Shannon conquered it. It robbed her of her physical strength, but never of her determination. It stole her mobility, but not her heart. It even deprived her of her beautiful hair, but it did not touch her dignity. The Bible says in 1 Corinthians 15:57, "But thanks be to God, who gives us the victory through our Lord Jesus Christ." This evening, Shannon became the victor and nothing harmful will ever bother her again (Revelation 21:4).

Where Was God?

(Note: I wrote the following soon after Shannon's passing. It was printed in the program that was handed out at her memorial service. - M.G.)

When facing life's trials, some begin to wonder if God is really there or, if He is, if He really cares about our suffering. Considering our frailty, such questioning is reasonable, so long as one searches for the answer and doesn't just throw his hands up in disgust and conclude that God does not exist. Job, Habakkuk, Asaph (Psalm 73) and others engaged in this type of thinking when they were facing difficulties. As we consider the question in this article's title, I hope that you will indulge me in my personal references. Their usage is the best way I know of providing an answer.

Where was God…

- …when we learned that my wife, Shannon, had an aggressive cancer that had arisen suddenly and without warning?

- … when she nearly died of collapsed lungs caused by the cancer?

- … when our family was thrown into turmoil with emergency room visits followed by days and then weeks of hospital stays?

- … when we were told that the cancer was incurable and that the best we could aim for was to make her comfortable in her declining days?

- … when she lost her battle for life?

- … when she departed this world?

Now let me tell you where He was…

- …when we were told of her disease. He was in the same place as He had been the dozens of times in years past that she had previously gone to doctors for checkups and was pronounced healthy.

- …when she nearly died. He was in the same place as the day the world was blessed with her birth.

- …when we were experiencing the long days and nights of hospital stays. He was in the same place that He had been on the thousands of days in which we walked freely and in good health.

- … when we were told that the end for her was near. He was in the same place as He was the day that we fell in love and our world began.

- … when she lost her battle for life. He was in the same place that He was on the day that He gave His only begotten Son on the cross so that death would not have the victory over His faithful ones (1 Corinthians 15:55-58)

- … when she departed this world. He was in the same place that He was when He welcomed her into His family by virtue of her new birth in immersion in water for the forgiveness of sins (Ephesians 3:15; John 3:3,5).

In essence, the God whom some blame for their woes when they're in the throes of life's challenges is the same God who is often forgotten when things are going well. He has not moved. The apostle Paul said that He is not far from every one of us, adding, "For in him we live and move and exist" (Acts 17:27-28). God said, "I will never desert you, nor will I ever forsake you" (Hebrews 13:5). If, in our trials we feel that God is not there, it would be wise for us to consider the fact that it is we who have moved, not God. In life's darkness, thinking that God has forgotten us, we might find ourselves asking, "God, where are you?" but in life's good days, when we tend to forget God, perhaps He asks, "My child, where are you?"

Appendix
God's Plan of Salvation

The Bible teaches that you and I are sinners (Romans 3:10,23). As such, we are displeasing to God (Psalm 5:5). Our sins, like a brick wall, separate us from Jehovah (Isaiah 59:1,2). They separate us from the One who is going to judge this world, the one who has the power to cast us into eternal hell or take us into eternal glory in heaven at Judgment (Matthew 7:21-23; 25:31-46).

Certainly, all of us desire to avoid the punishment of hell and to go to heaven, but how can we accomplish this desire if we are sinners who stand separated from God? Were it not for the grace of God, we could not accomplish it at all (Matthew 19:25,26; Titus 2:11).

Ephesians 2:8 states, "For by grace you have been saved through faith; and that not of yourselves: it is the gift of God." That "gift of God" is "eternal life in Christ Jesus our Lord" (Romans 6:23). Prompted by His perfect love, God gave His only begotten Son, Jesus the Christ, as a sacrifice for our sins (John 3:16). The penalty for sin has to be paid. Because of God's grace and love, He does not want us to have to pay that penalty (though we hasten to mention that God's perfect justice demands that those who do not obey the Lord be punished – Deuteronomy 32:4; 2 Thessalonians 1:7-9). The blood of His Son that was shed on a cross on the hill of Calvary nearly 2000 years ago paid the price for sin.

Our sins CAN be forgiven. We CAN be pure in the sight of God IF we will be washed in the soul-saving blood of Christ that is made available to every sinner. But how are we washed in this blood? God's grace saves us, but His grace alone does not save. It is by His grace that everyone has the opportunity to be saved, and it is by His grace that some will be saved, but not everyone will be saved in eternity (Matthew 7:13,14). Only those who obey the Lord's Gospel and thus are washed in the blood of Christ have the hope of eternal life (Revelation 1:5).

Again, referring to Ephesians 2:8, we learn that faith plays a part in our salvation. By His grace, God provides salvation, but WE must do something to receive it. We must believe (have faith) not only in Him (Hebrews 11:6), but also in Jesus as the Christ, the Son of God (John 8:24). BUT faith alone is not sufficient to save us from our sins (James 2:24). James 2:19 says that the devils believe, but they are not saved. Faith that is not put into action is a dead faith that is useless (James 2:20).

The New Testament very clearly tells us how to act on our faith so as to secure the blessing of forgiveness of sins. With the faith that we gained from God's Word, the Bible, firmly planted in our hearts and minds (Romans 10:17), we learn from the Bible of our sinful state. Knowing that we don't want to continue our lives as lost sinners, the next logical step for us to take is repentance. To repent means to change one's direction, to turn from one's devotion to Satan and turn to a devotion to God. Jesus stated that we all MUST repent (Luke 13:3). Peter indicated the same in Acts 2:38 and 3:19.

Faith and repentance are still not enough to secure Divine forgiveness. In the New Testament book of Acts, sometimes called the book of conversions, we have an example of a believing, penitent sinner making a public confession of Christ. "I believe that Jesus Christ is the Son of God," he declared. (Acts 8:37). Jesus had earlier stated that confession of belief in Him was necessary (Matthew 10:32,33). The apostle Paul later wrote that confession is made unto (in order to receive) salvation, "for the Scripture says, Whoever believes in Him will not be disappointed" (Romans 10:10,11).

Faith, repentance and confession still fall short of the blood of Christ. 2 Timothy 2:10 says that salvation is IN Christ Jesus. The alien sinner has to get INTO Christ somehow, but nowhere does the Bible say that we can believe into Christ. Nowhere does Sacred Scripture tell us that we can repent into Christ. The Divine record contains not one statement that says we can confess into Christ. How then can we get into Christ and be washed in the soul-cleansing blood of the Lamb of God (Hebrews 9:13,14)?

One passage of the Bible answers this question for us. Galatians 3:27 speaks of people who had been baptized (immersed) INTO Christ. Verse 28 speaks of them being IN Christ Jesus. They got there by virtue of their immersion into Christ.

The absolute necessity of immersion to be saved is taught in several New Testament passages (Mark 16:16; Acts 2:38; Acts 22:16; Romans 6:3ff; I Peter 3:21). This immersion is to be the one authorized by the Father, the Son, and the Holy Spirit in God's Word (Matthew 28:19). It is the one immersion mentioned in Ephesians 4:4-6, namely, immersion in water for the forgiveness of sins through the blood of Christ.

Faith which comes by hearing the Word of God (Romans 10:17), repentance, confession, and immersion for the remission of sins form man's part of being saved. These are not man-made works, for no one shall be saved by works that man creates (Ephesians 2:9). These are acts of obedience that God has mandated in His Word, acts that we MUST do if we want to break down the wall of sin that stands between us and Him.

Following these steps of salvation and rising up from the waters of immersion, not only is one a new creature (2 Corinthians 5:17), but he or she is then a member of the Lord's church, the one and ONLY one Jesus promised to build (Matthew 16:18). The Lord adds the saved to the church (Acts 2:47).

His church is not a denomination but is the one body into which all who want to be saved in eternity must come (Ephesians 1:22,23; 4:4-6; 5:23). Only those who have obeyed the Gospel and thus become members of the Lord's church can be called Christians (Acts 11:26).

Won't you, dear reader, look at the scriptures that have been cited, examine them carefully, and let them sink deeply into your heart? Won't you then muster the courage to obey the Lord? Your sins will be washed away. You will become a servant of the Lord (Romans 6:17,18) and a part of His family (Ephesians 3:10-15). You will have the hope of eternal life (Titus 1:1,2; I John 2:25). It's a hope that will become reality in Judgment if you will only continue to follow the Word of God exclusively all the days of your Christian life on earth (2 Timothy 4:7, 8; Hebrews 10:36). May God bless you as you do His will.

www.ingramcontent.com/pod-product-compliance
Lightning Source LLC
Chambersburg PA
CBHW060809120626
46557CB00001B/148